ritual

ritual

Magical Celebrations of Nature and Community from Around the World

NIKKI VAN DE CAR

ILLUSTRATED BY

BÁRBARA TAMILIN

RUNNING PRESS

PHILADELPHIA

Running Press
Hachette Book Group
1290 Avenue of the Americas, New York, NY 10104
www.runningpress.com
@Running_Press

Printed in Singapore

First Edition: March 2023

Published by Running Press, an imprint of Perseus Books, LLC,
a subsidiary of Hachette Book Group, Inc. The Running Press name and logo
are trademarks of the Hachette Book Group.

The Hachette Speakers Bureau provides a wide range of authors for speaking events.
To find out more, go to www.hachettespeakersbureau.com or call (866) 376-6591.

The publisher is not responsible for websites (or their content)
that are not owned by the publisher.

Print book cover and interior design by Susan Van Horn.

Library of Congress Control Number: 2022943388

ISBNs: 978-0-7624-8142-2 (hardcover), 978-0-7624-8143-9 (ebook)

COS

10 9 8 7 6 5 4 3 2 1

Contents

Introduction . . . 1

SPRING . . . 5

SUMMER . . . 43

FALL . . . 63

WINTER . . . 95

Conclusion . . . 133

Acknowledgments . . . 135

Index . . . 136

Introduction

NATURE IS WHAT GIVES US LIFE—IT IS THE SOURCE OF ALL magic and power in the world. This is something humans have understood since the beginning of time, and it is a constant among cultures around the world. However, the ways we celebrate nature and its inherent magic can vary wildly. Bulgarian Baba Marta Day welcomes the arrival of spring with martenitsi, little talismans of red and white string. In Southeast Asia, that same yearly event is celebrated during Holi, a joyful, riotous dance of colors. Yaldā, Soyal, Dongzhi, Inti Raymi, and Yule—from Iran, the American Southwest, China, Peru, and western Europe, respectively—are all very different, but each honors the winter solstice.

Each of these celebrations is a *ritual*—a form of magic created by community and tradition. While their differences can help us understand and celebrate varied cultural identities, their similarities can forge a bond that reaches across space and time. Now, this book can't possibly cover every single ritual celebration on earth, nor can it cover every aspect of these holidays—indeed, they are often incredibly complex and take on unique characteristics in different regions. The cultures that celebrate them aren't monoliths, and so there is a lot of variety in how the rituals are expressed from place to place and person to person. But we will look at the history and meaning behind forty of these ritual festivities, moving through the seasons as we honor and care for the magic in nature and one another. As you learn about these unique celebrations, you will find enchanted suggestions for how to participate in and appreciate them, without appropriating or laying claim to them.

If we can draw a broad conclusion about such wildly diverse magical celebrations, it is this: we are a part of the earth. All the folklore, gods and goddesses, rituals, foods, offerings, and celebrations boil down to gratitude for the earth—and for each other. We are not alone.

SPRING

SPRING IS A TIME OF RENEWAL, NEW BEGINNINGS, POSSIBILITY, and growth. It is when we step out from the darkness of winter and bask in the cool breeze and budding life around us. It is a jumping forward with new energy, and this remains true no matter where on earth you find yourself.

Most of the holidays in this chapter follow the Northern Hemisphere's vernal equinox, as cultures across the world recognize the impact astronomical events have on our daily lives. The ways in which we celebrate and understand this balance between day and night, this shift from winter to spring, can vary from culture to culture. Sometimes there is a story about the old becoming new or of rebirth. Often there are eggs involved. And so much of the time, there is joy, hope, and a sense of play—and isn't that what magic is all about?

SPRING CLEANING RITUAL

Cleaning may not sound particularly magical, but it can be one of the most empowering practices in your witchy life, partly because it involves taking something we do every day—or almost every day—and transforming it from the mundane into the marvelous.

Start with a sweeping spell. Work from the corners of your room, using your broom to gather dust, hair, and dirt tracked in from outside, as well as energy that has amassed, bringing it all to the center of the room. As you collect this debris in your dustpan, visualize the stagnant energy being swept up with it all. Of course, there is no dustpan on earth that lets us collect all of it—but that's all right. Gather what you can, and when you

dispose of it, let *everything* go—the dirt and detritus that has amassed literally in your home and metaphorically in your life. Release it.

Next, wash your windows. This is a chore that most of us don't do nearly often enough, and it's so important. It allows us to literally let in light and positivity. Use a mixture of equal parts white vinegar and water to scrub away all that has been blocking you, all that buildup around you. In cleansing your space, you are cleansing yourself.

See if you can go through all your various spring cleaning chores in the same way, using your intentions and your energy to unclog, clear, and remove everything that has grown dusty or stagnant, both within and without.

When you've finished, you can make a cleansing spray or use a diffuser with the following essential oils:

LEMON	**TEA TREE**	**MINT**
to symbolize light and the sun	for purifying	for clarity

Let their scents fill you as you breathe deeply and calmly, at peace in your space. You are ready to let in new energy and new possibilities.

EGG SPELL

There are a lot of magic spells that involve eggs, mostly in hoodoo and voodoo traditions from Haiti, the Caribbean, and the American South. In this instance, we are focusing on releasing and cleansing, the two major features of springtime celebrations.

Start by selecting an egg that feels good to you. Perhaps it represents where you are and where you have been. Is it white? Is it brown? Is it from a local farmer? Does it have a bit of roughness on the shell? Is it large or small? Go with your intuition.

Shake the egg, putting some energy into it as you do so. You're trying to break up the yolk and white—and symbolically, you're also trying to break up whatever has been stagnant within you. Take a pin and poke a hole into each end of the egg, both the flatter side and the pointier side. Wiggle your pin around to expand the holes a bit. Hold the egg over a bowl and let it drip out, blowing into one hole to force the egg through to the other side of the shell. You'll probably need to pause and shake some more, then go back to blowing over and over, repeating until the egg is completely empty.

Set the shell aside for now. The egg in your bowl represents all that you wanted to let go of, all that you wanted to push out and release. Pour the liquid out into a hole in the ground. Although you no longer need it, perhaps it can serve to nourish the earth.

Rinse out the shell under gently running water and then let it dry completely. This is now an empty vessel, full of possibility. You can leave it as is, perhaps adding it to an altar or nestling it into a found bird's nest. Or you can decorate it, using colors, symbols, and images that represent what you would like to invite into this newly open space in your life.

Chinese New Year

THE FIRST SOLAR TERM OF THE CHINESE CALENDAR; USUALLY BEGINS
AROUND FEBRUARY 4 AND ENDS AROUND FEBRUARY 19

The traditional Chinese calendar divides the year into twenty-four solar terms, and Lichun is the first. Lichun, which represents the beginning of spring, starts when the sun is at an angle of 315 degrees with the earth, and is followed by Yushui, which translates to "rainwater." Chinese New Year is celebrated with the arrival of Lichun.

According to legend, long ago the Nian, a mythical dragon who lived under the sea or in the mountains, would come to town to eat the villagers on the night of the new year. The villagers would hide, but one old man refused, fed up with the Nian and its devouring ways. He stayed up all night and put up red papers and set off firecrackers to scare the Nian away. It worked, and since then his success has been celebrated with the Chinese Lion Dance on the new year. There are New Year celebrations across East Asia, though their background and specifics can vary greatly.

Some cultures in East Asia celebrate the new year for the two weeks prior to Lichun. Like most springtime rituals, it starts with a good housecleaning, sweeping away ill-fortune to allow in the good. After cleaning, all brooms and dustpans are put away so that no one accidentally sweeps up the coming good luck.

There's a kind of spiritual and relational housecleaning, as well, as all debts are paid off before Lichun. And not just monetary debts, either—favors are repaid as well, often in the form of gifts and rice sent to colleagues. Gods and ancestors are honored with gifts, altar work, and prayer.

Then the doors and windows are decorated with intricate red paper cutouts. People also hang couplets—short, two-line poems of happiness and good fortune. The night of the celebration, family members gather for a big reunion dinner, enjoying dumplings, chicken, and pork, as well as fish. A number of traditionally included dishes are served because their names are homophones for good fortune.

After dinner, firecrackers are lit outside, to frighten away the Nian and other evil spirits. Then the doors to the household remain closed until morning, keeping any negative energy sealed out. Some people will stay up late at night, even past midnight, in the belief that keeping awake on this night will help their elders live longer.

Lichun is celebrated across East Asia as the beginning of spring, and here its rituals involve eggs, too.

Fresh chicken eggs are decorated for Lichun, and people will attempt to balance these beautiful objects on the broad end. Some believe that you can balance an egg only on certain days of the year. In Taiwan, that day falls on the fifth day of the fifth month of the Chinese calendar, the day of the Dragon Boat Festival. In the United States, it's believed an egg will balance only on the equinox, when day and night are also in balance.

In truth, an egg will balance on its broad end all year long—but it's never easy to do. In 1947, physicist Ukichiro Nakaya practiced with egg after egg and found that if you could triangulate three flaws—bumps or dimples—in the eggshell, you could turn the egg until you could orient between those flaws and help the egg remain upright no matter what day it was. Still, successfully balancing an egg on Lichun is said to bring good health and good fortune in the coming year.

WAYS TO CELEBRATE

- Decorate your home with red paper cutouts and write short couplets to invite good fortune in the coming year.

- Invite family members over for dinner, especially those you don't get to see very often.

- Try to balance an egg on its end! If you're having trouble, you could sprinkle some salt on the table to give it something to hang on to, and then carefully blow away the excess salt.

Têt

THE ARRIVAL OF SPRING IN THE VIETNAMESE CALENDAR,
USUALLY JANUARY OR FEBRUARY

Têt is short for Têt Nguyên Dán, which means "Festival of the First Morning of the First Day." The arrival of spring marks the new year in Vietnam, and similar to Chinese New Year festivities, it is a time to celebrate family.

In the days leading up to Tết, it is tradition to visit the graves of your ancestors, paying your respects and making sure the tombs are clean and well-kept. Then, it's back home to clean house and cook up a bunch of tasty foods for a big family meal, including broths and banh chung or sticky rice cakes. Houses are decorated with apricot blossoms, peach blossoms, and Saint-John's-wort. Those celebrating will often create a cây nêu, a tall tree made of a bamboo pole decorated with bows, arrows, bells, paper fish, and other good luck charms. It is wrapped in red paper to ward off evil spirits.

The sentiments behind celebrations of Tết are joyful, but also a little wistful. There is a sense of letting go of the troubles of the previous year and looking for a new start. The first day of Tết is spent just with parents and children, and the children are given red envelopes of money, to which they say, "Song lâu tram tuoi," which translates to "a long life of 100 years!" The children will play traditional games, including a dice game called bâu cua cá cop.

No one comes by to visit without first receiving an invitation, as the belief is that the first visitor a family receives will determine their fortune in the next year—which is a lot of pressure! So it is an honor to be the first person invited into a house at Tết—such a person is selected for their sense of honor, success, and kindness. The luck they bring with them is so valued that no one sweeps the floor during Tết, as they might sweep the good luck away.

Over the next two days, people visit relatives, friends, and teachers, who are traditionally highly respected in Vietnam. There are parades in which everyone ventures out into the streets, clanging gongs and bells, banging on drums, and lighting fireworks to make as much noise as possible to scare away any evil spirits. There will also be a Mua Lan, or the lion-dragon, who will dance through the streets, frightening spirits with his strength.

WAYS TO CELEBRATE

◆ Welcome the spring with a clamor! Bang on some drums and ring some bells! It is an exciting time and a return to life and, ideally, to good fortune.

◆ Choose a person to invite over to celebrate Têt, someone whose friendship you value, and let them know what this invitation symbolizes.

◆ Consider how to make a new start and how to let go of whatever troubles you've been carrying, making room for luck and happiness.

Baba Marta Day

MARCH 1

Baba Marta is a character of Bulgarian folklore, a fiery figure who, like the rest of us, is impatient with her brothers January and February. When Granny March does her spring cleaning and shakes out her mattress, the feathers that fall are the last snowfall of the year.

Of course, we've all been hopeful that one particular snowfall will be the last and been disappointed when another falls. So, on March 1, people in Bulgaria and some parts of Serbia exchange something called martenitsi on Baba Marta Day. These little bracelets are made of red and white yarn on which little thread dolls are strung—a man made of white string, Pizho, and a red-dressed woman, Penda. Together, red and white symbolize good health, with white standing for purity and red for life and passion. A martenitsa may also symbolize the melting snow and the rising sun in balance.

A martenitsa must always be given as a gift, not made or bought for yourself. You can wear it around the wrist or the neck or pin it to a jacket. As soon as you see a sign of spring, whether that's a bird returning north, a tree blossoming, or a flower poking up from the ground, then Baba Marta is in a good mood at last, and spring is truly here.

At that point, the martenitsa is removed. It can be tied onto a fruit tree to pass its good health on to the plant. Or it can be placed beneath a rock, and the creature that is found under the rock chosen can foretell how the coming year will go: If it is a worm, then the crops will be good. If it is an ant, then your hard work will pay off.

WAYS TO CELEBRATE

- Make your own martenitsi to give and share with others! They can be quite simple, and Pizho and Penda can hang from them like little charms.

- Watch for signs of spring, and be sure to place your martenitsa with care, whether it is hung on a tree or tucked beneath a stone.

- Shake out your blankets and mattresses to signal that you are ready for the last snowfall.

Holi

THE FULL MOON DAY IN THE MONTH OF PHALGUNA,
THE TWELFTH MONTH OF THE HINDU CALENDAR

The Hindu Festival of Colors is one of the most joyful celebrations in the world. It's largely observed in India and Nepal, but can be found throughout Asia and across Europe and North America, as well. As with all such widespread ritual celebrations, it can vary a great deal from place to place and culture to culture.

But, in general, it celebrates the eternal and divine love of Radha and Krishna. According to legend, Krishna feared that Radha would not love him in return, because she was light-skinned and he was dark. His mother, Yashoda, told him to color Radha however he wanted—and so he did. The ritual color play of Holi is to commemorate that moment.

Holi is also about the triumph of good over evil, found in the victory of Vishnu over Hiranyakashipu, a demon king who could not be killed—not by a human or an animal, indoors nor outdoors, at day or night, by handheld or projectile weapons, on land or in the air. Hiranyakashipu demanded worship, but his son Prahlada remained devoted to Vishnu, which enraged his father. Holika, Prahlada's aunt and Hiranyakashipu's sister, tricked Prahlada into sitting on a pyre with her. She wore a magic cloak that would protect her while Prahlada burned—but the cloak betrayed her, flying to Prahlada and leaving Holika to burn on her own pyre. Vishnu came to Hiranyakashipu in the lion-human form of Nara-simha (so he was neither human nor animal) and met him on the door-step (neither indoors nor out) at dusk (neither day nor night). Vishnu took him in his lap (which isn't land or in the air) and killed Hiranyaka-shipu with his lion's claws, which weren't weapons at all.

The celebration of Holi begins the night before with Holika Dahan, a burning in effigy of the demon Holika. This ritual symbolizes the purifica-tion and burning away of all the evils that the celebrants carry, everything they have picked over the course of the year. And in the morning, it's party time! Think of your wildest water balloon or water gun fights from child-hood, and then toss in a rainbow of color. Everyone is fair game—friends and strangers, adults, children, and even the elderly. There is music and dancing and general raucous, joyous mayhem. By the end of the day, every single person looks like a brightly hued walking work of art.

More than anything, Holi celebrates the arrival of spring. It is a time to play and laugh, to repair broken relationships, and to forgive and forget. Conflicts can be set aside and all the pain that we have been carrying can be let go in favor of joy and love. At the end of the day, everyone cleans up and gets dressed up to visit friends and relatives, cementing connections.

While some commercially made pigments have become popular due to their ease and availability, traditionally the colors of Holi have come from plants and had healing properties, rooted as they are in the Ayurvedic tradition.

ORANGE AND RED
are frequently derived from the flowers of the tesu tree, known as "the flame of the forest." Sandalwood, dried hibiscus, madder, radish, saffron, and pomegranate powders can also provide bright reds and oranges.

GREEN
can be made from a mixture of mehndi (henna) and the dried leaves of the gulmohur tree, or from fresh leaves and herbs.

YELLOW
is most often made with turmeric powder, sometimes mixed with chickpea flour. Dried marigolds and chrysanthemums also provide a good yellow pigment.

BLUE
is achieved with indigo, an excellent source of blue pigment, as well as blue hibiscus and jacaranda flowers.

PURPLE
can come from beets, which offer a good magenta or purple shade, particularly when boiled.

BROWN
pigment can come from dried tea leaves or from clay.

BLACK
pigment can be derived from gooseberries, grapes, and charcoal.

WAYS TO CELEBRATE

◆ Light a bonfire meant to burn away all that you have been carrying—whatever you feel you don't need to take with you into the spring.

◆ Have a colorful water fight! Make sure you use natural and nontoxic dyes, and avoid the eyes. But otherwise, let loose! Feel the joy and abandon that Holi is meant to celebrate.

◆ Make sure the people who are most important to you know it. If you can, try to forgive someone—or yourself—or simply release any resentments. Start over.

Nowruz

THE SPRING EQUINOX

In Persian, Nowruz translates to "New Day"—and it falls on the spring equinox as the first day of the Persian, or Iranian, New Year. Like all celebrations of the new year, Nowruz symbolizes fresh beginnings, an apt intention for a holiday that coincides with the first day of spring, when life begins again.

Nowruz has been widely celebrated for over 3,000 years, across Asia and around the Black Sea and the Balkans. For the most part, it's a secular celebration of nature, though for some Muslims, Zoroastrians, and Bahá'ís, Nowruz is a holy day.

Because Nowruz is celebrated by so many different people in so many different countries, it can vary significantly from place to place. In Azerbaijan, every Tuesday in the month before Nowruz there is a festival celebrating the four elements—earth, wind, fire, and water. Most people begin to prepare for Nowruz well in advance, doing a heavy spring cleaning known as khane tekani and decorating with flowers, usually hyacinths and tulips.

Chaharshanbe Suri is the eve of the last Wednesday before Nowruz, and it is a night filled with fireworks and jumping over bonfires. Celebrants in Iran might sing "My yellow is yours, your red is mine" to the fire, asking it to take away any ill-health and replace it instead with the fire's warmth, vigor, and energy.

After the bonfire celebration, you might fill a clay pot or jug with something that symbolizes any bad luck that might come with the new year, before swinging it around to capture all potential misfortune and then hurling it off the roof of the house, smashing it in the street below. The celebration may also include spoon-banging, a custom much like trick-or-treating, only more raucous—people dressed in disguises bang on pots and pans with spoons in exchange for treats.

Chaharshanbe Suri is also an opportunity to visit and tend the graves of relatives and to set up a Haft-sin table. This is an arrangement of seven symbolic items whose Persian names all begin with the letter *sin*.

1. **SABZEH**—wheat, barley, mung bean, or lentil sprouts grown in a dish, to symbolize renewal

2. **SAMANU**—wheat germ sweet pudding, to symbolize prosperity

3. **SENJED**—oleaster, for love

4. **SERKEH**—vinegar, for patience

23

⑤ **SEER**—garlic, for health

⑥ **SOMĀQ**—sumac, for sunrise

⑦ **SEEB**—apple, for beauty

The table may also include a book of wisdom reflective of the celebrant's faith (like the Quran, the Bible, the Avesta, etc.), coins, hyacinths, a clock, a mirror, candles, painted eggs, goldfish, and Persian treats.

Speaking of treats, Nowruz also features a figure called Ama Nowruz, the husband of Nane Sarma, also known as "Grandma Frost." Their love is a difficult one, as they can only meet on this one night—the night when Grandma Frost leaves this world, surrendering to the coming warmth of spring. But Amu Nowruz is so excited to see her that, together with his dancing and singing companion Haji Firuz, he brings gifts for all the children.

WAYS TO CELEBRATE

◆ A deep spring cleaning is always a good idea! Get at those places you normally don't bother with, like the baseboards and behind the refrigerator, and clean your windows to let in the warmer light. Do so with intention—the root of all magic.

◆ Set up a kind of Haft-sin table that feels right to you for the place and culture where you live. Perhaps you can collect seven items that have similar meanings for you and create an altar to spring inspired by Nowruz.

◆ Decorate with flowers! Say farewell to Nane Sarma with a loving spring send-off.

Mesoamerican Spring Equinox

THE SPRING EQUINOX

Teotihuacán is an ancient Mesoamerican city in Mexico. Its name loosely translates to "birthplace of the gods." The site contains several pyramids, including the immense Pyramid of the Sun, the third largest pyramid in the world.

Every year, thousands of people gather at the base of the Pyramid of the Sun to celebrate the spring equinox. Traditionally, they all dress in white, perhaps accented with a red scarf. People dance and burn incense, and most climb to the top of the pyramid. It takes 360 steps to reach the top, and if you get there at daybreak, you can watch as the sun rises over the Apan Mountains to the east, arms outstretched to greet it.

Near the Pyramid of the Sun rests the Palace of Quetzalcoatl. Quetzal-coatl is the Nahuatl name for the Feathered-Serpent deity of Mesoamerican culture, and his Yucatec Mayan equivalent is known as Kukulcán. The feathers of Quetzalcoatl represent his divine nature—including his ability to fly—but his serpent aspect grounds him on earth.

On the equinox, light from the rising sun casts a shadow along figures etched and painted in red on the west wall of the Palace of Quetzalcoatl. It is only on this morning that the shadow follows this line so perfectly. The figures include owls, which would have symbolized darkness, as well as rays of light. Equinoxes are fully balanced, with the length of the day being equal to that of the night, and it seems likely that these figures illustrate that balance, the same one that Quetzalcoatl embodies.

There is a similar celebration at Chichen Itza, another ancient city in Mexico. There is a spectacle at the Temple of Kukulcán that occurs on both the spring and fall equinoxes—as the sun begins to set, it casts a shadow atop the pyramid, followed by another, and another, so that it appears there is a snake is sliding down the staircase of the pyramid. That shadow-snake connects with the statue of the feathered serpent at the bottom of the pyramid and rests there for about forty-five minutes before disappearing.

WAYS TO CELEBRATE

◆ Create shadow art of your own inspired by the light show at Chichen Itza or by the shadowed drawings at the Palace of Quetzalcoatl.

◆ Consider how to find balance in your own life, as Quetzalcoatl represents earth and sky, light and dark.

◆ Wear white, perhaps accented with red, to invite the healing energy of the sun.

Ostara

THE SPRING EQUINOX

The celebrations of the equinox found in Wiccan or druidic traditions are known as Ostara, or Alban Eilir. There are a number of deities honored on this day, including Eostre, a goddess of spring. She's a somewhat mysterious goddess—it's unknown who exactly worshipped her or even necessarily what she represented. Jacob Grimm, collector of fairy tales, theorized that she was a "divinity of the radiant dawn, of upspringing light," which is a delightful image perfect for the spring equinox.

At some point, Eostre became associated with eggs and rabbits—note the linguistic similarity between Eostre and Easter—and with fertility.

If we think about the golden orb of the yolk as sun energy (traditionally viewed as masculine) and the amorphous white as moon energy (traditionally viewed as feminine), then the egg is balanced within itself, just as the day and night are in balance on the equinox. Certain legends centered around this time tell the story of a rabbit that could turn into a bird . . . which may be why the Easter Bunny leaves eggs for collection. As it happens, rabbits are often associated with the moon and fertility across a variety of cultures around the world. In this way, Ostara brings together the goddess of the dawn and the light of the moon.

While Ostara, like all spring equinox rituals, celebrates the balance between the day and night, it is more focused on Eostre's association with fertility. In this celebration, the symbolism of an egg is that of potential— of new life and rebirth. Spring is here at last: new leaves are sprouting, the chill is leaving the air, and from here on out the sun will be brighter. The upspringing light has come.

WAYS TO CELEBRATE

◆ Coloring and collecting Easter eggs is a wonderful way to celebrate Ostara, and in all likelihood, celebrating Ostara has been what you were doing all along.

◆ Grimm also referred to baked goods made on Ostara as "pastry of heathenish form," which is another delightful turn of phrase. You could make hot cross buns, or Easter Bread with colorful eggs snuggled in its twists.

◆ One theory behind hot cross buns is that the cross will keep the devil out of your bread. You could maintain a balance by making deviled eggs to accompany them.

Songkran

APRIL 13

The word *Songkran* is derived from the Sanskrit term for "astrological passage," specifically the sun's shift from Pisces into Aries. This is the new beginning of the zodiac, though the history of this festival is related to Buddhist lore, rather than astrology. The story is of a clever and good boy named Thammabal. So clever was he that Kapila Brahma—a figure from Hindu religious tradition who had a profound impact on Buddhism—wanted to test him. He asked, "Where is the *sri,* the glory of men found in the morning, during the day, and in the evening?"

Thammabal could not find the answer to his riddle—until that is, while resting beneath a palm tree, he overheard two eagles discussing how they would eat him when he failed the test. The cost of getting it wrong was his head. The eagles knew the answer—the sri appeared on the face in the mornings, when people wash their faces. It is on the chest at noon, when people douse themselves with perfume. And it is on the feet at night, when people wash their feet at the end of the day.

Thammabal gave this answer to Kapila Brahma. And since he got it right, Kapila Brahma was the one who had to lose his head. But he wasn't sure how to do this—if his head fell to the earth, there would be a firestorm of such magnitude the whole world would burn. If he threw it into the air, the rains would stop and the crops would die. And if he dropped it into the ocean, the seas would dry up.

So Kapila Brahma's daughters placed his severed head on a phan, a ceremonial tray, which was then kept in Mount Kailash in Tibet. Every year since then, on the day the sun enters Aries, one of Kapila Brahma's children honors him by carrying the phan that holds his head. In the morning she stands, with her sri at her face. At noon she sits, with her sri at chest level. And at night she lays down, at the height of feet, though she does not sleep until midnight.

The morning of Songkran begins with merit-making—the practice of giving food or other offerings to Buddhist monks to increase their good karma. This practice is by no means limited to Songkran, but it is a good day for it. And then there is the ritual purification by water, perhaps out of relief that Kapila Brahma's head did not remove all the water from the world. Statues of Buddha are rinsed with water, as are the young and the elderly, to wash away any ill luck.

The purification could have been a simple sprinkling with water, but this ritual has grown boisterous and joyous—a full-on water festival. Streets are closed down, and everyone—old, young, and everything in between—splashes water on each other in the world's biggest water fight. Buckets, water guns, and even pressure hoses are employed to make sure absolutely everyone is drenched.

WAYS TO CELEBRATE

◆ Do some merit-making! You can certainly donate food to a nearby Buddhist monastery, or you can find a homeless shelter, food basket, or other place that can help make sure your donations get to the people who need them.

◆ Get in touch with relatives you haven't spoken with in a while— one of the main functions of Songkran is to remind us of the importance of family.

◆ Have a good old-fashioned raucous water fight!

Sham el-Nessim

THE MONDAY AFTER EASTER

Sham el-Nessim translates to "inhaling the breeze," which is a lovely way to think about taking a pause to acknowledge the change in season and to prepare for the work to come. The original Coptic name was Tshom Ni Tshom, which means "garden meadows."

Although this Egyptian holiday is scheduled for the Monday following Easter, it is actually entirely secular, with no religious significance. In fact, it is one of the oldest known spring festivals, having been celebrated since at least 2700 BCE. Activities are limited, mostly centering around going to the beach or the park or simply sitting outdoors, picnicking on salted fish and lettuce and enjoying that pause, that spring-scented breeze. There may be dancing and music and other relaxing, joyful ways to spend the day.

However, celebrants do take the time to color eggs! Given the ancient history of this holiday, it's likely that Sham el-Nessim is where the practice originated, before spreading throughout the world. In Egypt, as elsewhere, eggs symbolize rebirth and new beginnings. The eggs are boiled and dyed, and then decorated with written wishes. They are then given to others, or they are hung in baskets outside, casting the wishes on the wind.

WAYS TO CELEBRATE

- The restful, simplistic nature of this holiday means that you can celebrate it simply by taking a pause. Sit outside and inhale the breeze, setting an intention for how you will engage with the coming spring season.

- Go outside and have a picnic! Lay out on the blankets, looking for leaves just budding in the trees above you.

- Write wishes on your eggs and leave them outside for a day or so to see what they invite.

Qingming Festival

THE FIFTEENTH DAY AFTER THE SPRING EQUINOX

Qingming falls on the first day of the fifth solar term of the traditional Chinese calendar, usually on April 4, 5, or 6. It has been observed for over 2,500 years and was originally simply a celebration of the change in season—*Qingming* translates to "clearness" or "brightness."

But then the meaning shifted, due perhaps to a legend about Prince Chong'er. The winter was hard, and Prince Chong'er was about to starve to death. To save him, his loyal companion Jie Zitui made him a soup using meat from his own thigh, though he did not tell Prince Chong'er where the meat had come from. When Chong'er had recovered and discovered what Jie had done, he swore to properly reward him someday.

Nineteen years later, Prince Chong'er came into power as Duke Wen of Jin. When he went at last to reward Jie Zitui with a title, Jie did not want it and hid in the mountains with his mother. In a rather questionable attempt to confer his gratitude, Duke Wen set fire to the mountain to force Jie out of hiding. Three days later, the bodies of Jie Zitui and his mother were found in a cave under a willow tree on the mountain. Duke Wen buried them with all ceremony. In honor of Jie's long-ago sacrifice, he ordered his subjects not to use fire and to only eat cold food on that day. The next year, the willow tree had recovered from the fire, and Duke Wen swept the tomb. Since then, Qingming has begun with a Cold Food Day, when no food is cooked or heated, and ends with ritual tomb-sweeping to honor the ancestors.

In the thousands of years since then, people across China have visited burial grounds and swept tombs on this day. In some places, this is the only day this kind of maintenance occurs, as it is believed that sweeping will disturb the dead if it is done on any other day.

The honoring of ancestors is less about worship and more about respect and reverence for family, though tomb-sweeping is quite a complex set of rituals. Family members kneel down to offer prayer and respect before burning incense sticks or silver-leafed paper. The tomb is swept clean, and offerings of spirit money, food, tea, and wine are left in memory of the ancestors. Many may also offer their respects to important historical or political figures.

Much in the same way that palm leaves are carried on Easter Sunday in certain Christian traditions, some Chinese people may carry symbols of ritual purity, like pomegranates or willow branches, while observing Qingming. Like many rites of spring, this celebration is also a time for couples to begin courting. It is also a significant milestone in Chinese tea culture, as it is the dividing line between certain green teas. Leaves picked before this date are prized for their lighter, subtler scent and flavor.

After the work of the day is done, families will often go out in the evening and fly kites, tying little colored lanterns to them so they twinkle like stars in the twilight. In the past, some would cut the string to let the kite fly, inviting good luck and warding off illness, though this custom has fallen out of favor for the same reasons the releasing of balloons is discouraged—the detritus has to fall somewhere.

WAYS TO CELEBRATE

◆ Visit your own ancestors, honoring them and tending their graves in a way that feels right for you and your culture. Connecting with family and the past is always important.

◆ Enjoy some green tea—maybe even pre-Qingming tea if you can find it—sipping it with reverence for the work that has gone into it and the growth of the leaves, as well as the harvest.

◆ Fly a kite in the evening! If you can figure out how to attach a lantern to your kite, see it sparkle above you.

Beltane

MAY 1

This end of spring celebration dates back to the Floralia, an ancient Roman festival that was a bit more pleasure-seeking and passionate than most—a flavor that has stayed with this ritual through its many incarnations. Maiouma, the ancient Greek version, was a celebration of Dionysus and Aphrodite, the gods of pleasure and love, respectively, so you can imagine the kinds of rites that supposedly went along with that.

As these Greek and Roman traditions made their way across Europe, the ways in which they were interpreted shifted to match the beliefs of the cultures they encountered. It is perhaps not surprising that when these licentious celebrations clashed with Christianity, some of the messaging went a little awry. In Germanic countries, May 1 is celebrated as Walpurgis, in dedication to St. Walpurga who saved her people from witchcraft. But given that May 1 was the day she had to do the saving, during the Renaissance it was believed that Walpurgis night was when evil was at its strongest. According to German folklore, witches would meet on the highest peak in the Harz Mountains to cast their spells or suchlike. The villagers would then light bonfires to drive them away.

In Portugal, May Day was equally focused on the potential of evil, as Maias was also known as Dia das Bruxas, or Witches' Day. The yellow flowers of the broom plant were placed on all entryways, including doors, windows, and later even in cars to protect them from witches.

But in Gaelic and Celtic cultures, Floralia became known as Beltane, which translates to "lucky fire." All household fires would be doused and the Beltane bonfire would be lit in each village, often by the most rudimentary and labor-intensive methods possible, to increase its power. A "needfire" was made by rubbing two sticks together, and it was from this small flame that all the other fires had to be kindled.

For Beltane, the bonfires were meant to be leaped over, both for luck and for protection from fairies. Cattle in particular were forced to jump over the fire, as May 1 was the day they were sent back out to pasture after the cold of winter—so they needed the protection of the flames. When the fires burned down in the morning, the ashes would be sprinkled on the crops.

Offerings were made to the fairies, often in the form of bannocks—small oatcakes made in the flames of the bonfire. Yellow flowers, including primrose, rowan, gorse, and hazel, were placed in doors and windows to evoke the protective nature of fire.

By the mid-eighteenth century, Christianity had found its way into Beltane, and the celebration became Mary's Day. During this festival, statues of Mary were crowned with flowered wreaths and participants danced around a maypole—though no one quite knows the symbolism of that. Nowadays, May Queens are crowned with Mary's wreaths. The Beltane Fire Festival is still held in Edinburgh, and some women still climb Arthur's Seat, a possible location of Camelot found in the hills outside the city. On May 1, anyone who washes her face in the morning dew there will remain beautiful for life, rendering skin care products unnecessary.

At some point—likely during the rise of Neo-paganism movements—Beltane reached back to its passionate and pleasure-seeking origins in Floralia. Couples that had been married for a year and a day could remove their wedding rings on this night, and for that night alone be single once again—with all the freedom that implies.

WAYS TO CELEBRATE

◆ Hang yellow flowers in your entryways, both for protection and luck.

◆ Create a maypole and weave a dance around it! It's surprisingly challenging to do it "right" and quite a lot of fun.

◆ Light a bonfire—even a needfire, if you can!—though perhaps don't jump over it. You can, however, bake a bannock as an offering to the fairies.

Great Dragon Parade

END OF MAY–EARLY JUNE

Kraków was founded by Krakus, a legendary Polish hero—or antihero, depending on which version you read. Near the Vistula River dwelled the Wawel Dragon, a creature that required weekly offerings of cattle, lest it steal the village maidens instead. A cobbler named Krak came up with a Trojan horse idea—he stuffed a sheep full of sulfur and mustard seeds and left it outside the dragon's cave. When the dragon ate the sheep, he roared in pain and rushed to the river. He drank so much he drained the Vistula dry—at which point he exploded. Krak was crowned a hero and became King Krakus. He then built Wawel Castle over the dragon's cave.

Older versions of the tale say that Krakus and his brother Lech killed the dragon together, after which Krakus killed his brother so he could rule alone—the cobbler-turned-king is a more modern take, albeit a much happier one.

Wawel Castle still stands on Wawel Hill, and next to it is Wawel Cathedral. At the entrance to the cathedral are bones from the Pleistocene epoch, once believed to have been those of the Wawel Dragon. The bones hang on a chain, and it's believed that as long as they hang there, the world will carry on.

In 1969, artist Bronislaw Chromy built a sculpture of the Wawel Dragon. It stands outside the cathedral and is complete with natural gas fire that it breathes at passersby.

Every year, residents of Kraków celebrate the defeat of the Wawel Dragon. Children from all over Poland create dragon sculptures and march in a parade of handmade dragons, following larger sculptures that can be seventy-five feet long and forty-five feet high—plenty big enough to swallow an entire river.

WAYS TO CELEBRATE

◆ Make a dragon sculpture of your own!

◆ Perhaps organize a small parade of friends and family, each with their own dragon sculptures.

◆ Look up stories of dragons in your area—just about every culture on earth has them. Maybe you've been dwelling among dragons, too.

SUMMER

THE CELEBRATIONS OF SUMMER TEND TO CENTER AROUND the summer solstice, though the majority of them don't actually fall *on* the solstice, but a few days later. In many parts of the world this is due to a shift away from the harvest- and seasonal-focused rituals of paganism toward the purely spiritual-focused rituals of Christianity. Like the relationship between Ostara and Easter, the festivities of summer became celebrations of Christian figures.

However, there are still echoes of pagan traditions within these holidays—and some of those echoes are extremely loud! The focus of most of these is on fun, relationships—particularly romantic ones—and family. After all, summer is the most vibrant, lush, and energetic time of year. It is a period to bask in the radiance of the earth and each other, feeling the exchange of energy and power that we all share, no matter where we are.

FLOWER DYEING SPELL

This spell produces a physically crafted object, something you can wear or use to decorate for your summer celebrations. You'll need an undyed cloth—you can use white cloth napkins or a table runner, a white silk scarf, a white apron, or anything else that feels like something you would use and that would bring you joy. You'll also need a hammer, some white vinegar, and some string or thread. If you want to be able to wash your cloth without it fading, soak it in a mordant like aluminum sulfate before dyeing.

Start by going out and gathering flowers. You can buy them from the store if you don't have a handy field of wildflowers nearby, but you'd be surprised at how many flowers you can find just walking around in the summer, even in a city. Look for the brightest and most vibrant colors you can find, and get enough to cover roughly half of your chosen fabric.

When you're ready, get your fabric soaking wet, then lay it down flat. Scatter your chosen blossoms over half of the fabric, putting some intention into how you arrange them. What does each flower represent for you? What do the colors mean? As you place each flower, reflect on something that it brings up for you, something that gives you joy.

When you're satisfied with your arrangement, fold the fabric in half, covering up the blossoms. Take your hammer and tap on each flower, releasing its juices and allowing its color to bleed into the fabric. You are imbuing your cloth with the essence of these blooms. When each flower has been pounded into place, fold and roll your fabric into a tight little bundle, rather like an herbal bundle used for smoke cleansing and purification. Take your string or thread and wrap it tightly, keeping the flowers in place.

Bring a small pot of water just to a simmer, adding some white vinegar to help the color set. Place your bundle inside, and let it steep for about an hour, then turn off the heat and allow it come to room temperature.

When it's ready, remove the bundle and squeeze it softly. Snip your strings and gently unfurl the cloth, removing the now dull flowers and revealing the colors they have left behind. Give the cloth a gentle rinse and let it hang dry. Whenever or however you use it, let each splash of color remind you of what the flowers meant to you, giving you their joy and energy.

LOVE SPELL

Summer love can mean a lot of things. It can mean a sweet, breezy romance. It can mean a barbecue in the park with family and friends. It can mean lying on a blanket under a tree, reading and basking in your own company. Before beginning this spell, consider what kind of love you would like to feel this summer. What kind of loving warmth do you wish to invoke?

Gather some wild water, either from a river, a pond, or a puddle of rain left over from a summer thunderstorm. Pour it into a jar and add a few drops of honey, some green leaves—oak leaves, if they're available—and a scattering of flower petals. With each ingredient, set your intentions for the love you will embody—the sweetness and beauty of it, and the energy and care it will give you. If you like, add a crystal like rose quartz or malachite to resonate with that loving energy.

Seal your jar and place it on your desk, near your bed, or on your altar if you have one—anywhere that's visible, so that it can be a part of your life, reminding you of the love you create for yourself, every day.

Litha

THE SUMMER SOLSTICE

Like Beltane, the summer solstice is celebrated in a wide variety of ways across Europe. On this longest day of the year the sun is at its closest to the earth, and it is a time to bask in its warmth and life. The term *Litha* comes from Celtic traditions in Ireland and Scotland. According to folklore, Litha is the day on which the battle between light and dark reaches its peak.

The Oak King rules the warmer, lighter months, while the Holly King is the lord of winter—these two are eternally at war for supremacy of the wheel of the year. According to one version of the tale, the Oak King conquers the Holly King on Ostara (see page 27), reaches the height of his powers on Litha, and then loses to the Holly King on Mabon (see page 74), the autumn equinox. The Holly King then reaches the height of his own powers on Yule (see page 109), the winter solstice, in a remarkably apt and direct interpretation of the seasons as mythical figures.

The Oak King represents light and growth and is often associated with a fertility figure like the Green Man. This time of the Oak King is thought to be a good one for love, and so handfasting on Litha is a long-standing tradition.

Perhaps the best place to witness this honoring of the sun and light is at Stonehenge, in the Salisbury Plain of England. The rocks that make up this series of monoliths aren't from anywhere nearby—they were brought from 150 miles away, in what is now Wales. There are eighty of them, with some weighing up to twenty-five tons. The creation of this transcendent place was no mere whim carried out some 2,500 years ago—this was intentional and required a great deal of planning and work.

The stones are divided into two C-shapes facing each other, like an open circle with another open circle within it. We can't know exactly how Stonehenge originally worked or what it was for, as Litha traditions were broken up and all rituals done at the site these days are modern interpretations of what *may* have been practiced by druids long ago. But we do know that this location is aligned with both the summer and winter solstices. The Heel or Sun Stone lies at the northeast section of the outer circle. It is unusually rough in texture and leans toward the inner circle. A person standing before it within the center circle will see the sun rise over the Sun Stone on the dawn of the summer solstice.

Stonehenge is by no means the only architectural artifact in the world built around the solstice. The Temple of the Sun in Machu Picchu is the only structure in the Incan city that is circular in shape. There are small windows placed strategically so that during sunrise on the summer solstice (which is in December in Peru) these windows cast light directly on the altar placed in the center of the temple. Similarly, at Karnak Temple in Egypt, the summer solstice sun sets between the pillars of the western gate to shine into the inner sanctum of the temple of Amon-Ra, the ancient Egyptian sun god.

WAYS TO CELEBRATE

◆ Wake up early to watch the sun rise, welcoming the Oak King and enjoying all that he has to offer.

◆ Gather oak leaves to make a wreath to hang on your doorway or to wear as a crown.

◆ Go out into the woods to walk in the Oak King's realm, feeling your connection with all he represents.

Midsummer

JUNE 24

Sometime in the fourth century, European celebrations of the solstice melded with Christianity, shifting a couple of days away from the longest day and changing to a feast day for St. John the Baptist. This mirrors how celebrations of the birth of Jesus melded with and supplanted celebrations of Yule, the winter solstice, the longest night. Interestingly, a biblical text about the relationship between John the Baptist and Jesus Christ mirrors the storytelling around the Oak King and the Holly King: "He must increase, but I must decrease" (John 3:30).

As Christianity spread around the world, so did St. John's Day celebrations. They spread so widely that today two cities in Brazil—Caruaru and Campina Grande—compete for the title of biggest Festa Junina in the world. Celebrants dance the quadrilha around figures of a mock bride and groom in a callback to the handfasting traditions of Litha, and a maypole-esque pau-de-sebo is erected and danced around.

Across the world in Portugal, festivities are quite similar, though they have expanded to include the three main Saints' Days of June—St. Anthony and St. Peter, as well as St. John—so the celebration is called Santos Populares. Streets are decorated, altars dedicated to the saints are erected, and there is an abundance of good food. There is folk dancing and cantar à desgarrada, which is essentially an improvised-singing competition.

But in Eastern European countries, celebrations of Midsummer remain remarkably pagan, and they all seem to center around three main elements:

- ◆ **PLANTS**, either medicinal or magical in nature—frequently ferns, fennel, rue, rosemary, mallow, and of course, Saint-John's-wort. These may be arranged into a wreath, which may be hung in doorways, cast into a fire, or floated in water.

- ◆ **WATER.** Wild water comes into play, often in the form of dew collected at sunrise that morning.

- ◆ **FIRE.** St. John's Day celebrations almost always feature bonfires, and almost all Midsummer celebrations involve some kind of jumping across them—safely, of course!

In Bulgaria, the name of this festival is Enyovden, and it celebrates witches, healers, and fairies known as samodiva. Enyovden dates back to when women were the healers of their communities, and the belief was that the medicinal herbs they used in their work would be the most potent if gathered the night before this day. Women healers would venture out before sunrise to gather all the herbs they would need in the coming year.

Of course, the idea of women wandering around the woods in the dark has always translated to magic in some way, and so stories of witches and fairies wandering with them were inevitable. Today, the work of these women is honored when men and women alike venture out the night before Enyovden and collect seventy-seven and a half herbs—seventy-seven to heal all known illnesses, and that half herb to stand in for the unknown magical herb said to cure all illnesses. Those herbs are then woven into a wreath and hung on doors for protection and good health.

When the sun rises, its light dances and plays, as if it is bathing in the water. Swimming in lakes, rivers, or even splashing your face or eyelids with the morning dew is said to bring good health.

In Estonia, people jump over bonfires on Jaanipäev to avoid bad luck—and if you don't even light the fire, you are said to risk having your house catch fire as a consequence. In Finland, will-o'-the-wisps may appear, luring maidens into the forest to collect seven different flowers to place under their pillows so they can dream of their future husbands.

In Slavic countries, Midsummer is known as Ivan Kupala, a combination of St. John (Ivan) and Kupala, which was the name of a pagan fertility rite that took place around the solstice. Ivan Kupala manages to capture all three of the common elements of a Midsummer celebration. Couples jump over bonfires to prove their bravery and devotion, and if they don't complete the jump together, their relationship will not last.

Unattached women float wreaths of flowers, sometimes lit with candles, down rivers and then watch their path. Young men will often try to capture the wreathes, symbolically capturing the heart of the woman who released it.

It is believed that the eve of Ivan Kupala is the only time of year when ferns blossom. Of course, ferns are angiosperms and reproduce through their spores, but should a person find a fern in flower, they would receive luck, prosperity, and discernment. Believers would wander the woods in search of this flower in a very Shakespearean Midsummer night.

WAYS TO CELEBRATE

◆ Even if you can't find a will-o'-the-wisp to guide you, venture out into the forest to collect flowers, herbs, and ferns. You can create a wreath with them and hang it on your door or float it in a nearby stream or lake.

◆ Wake up at sunrise to bathe your face in the morning dew.

◆ Light a bonfire! But don't jump over it unless you're absolutely certain it's safe.

Vardavar

NINETY-EIGHT DAYS AFTER EASTER, USUALLY IN MID-JULY

Vardavar is a festival in Armenia that dates back to the pagan worship of the goddess Astghik, ruler of water, beauty, love, and fertility. At one time, she was considered the creator of the world, but over time Armenian folklore shifted to a more masculine interpretation and Aramazd became the creator, together with Anahit, a lunar maternal deity.

In a somewhat fitting form of vengeance for this demotion, Vardavar is celebrated by attacking unsuspecting passersby with water, splashing them with buckets or spray guns. It's likely that everyone involved—

except for tourists!—knows what is happening and gets in on the fun, particularly kids. It's a long day of water skirmishes that takes place across the country.

But as Armenia was one of the first countries to adopt Christianity as a national religion, the focus of Vardavar shifted away from Astghik, to a celebration of the transfiguration of Christ.

Family and ancestors are honored in Armenia, and on the day after Vardavar people will leave buckets of water by the graves of their loved ones, helping them to share in the joy and play of the day, even though they are not present.

WAYS TO CELEBRATE

- As with Songkran, there's nothing so fun as splashing each other with water on a hot day! But perhaps it's better not to involve unsuspecting strangers . . .

- Leave something joyful at the graves of your ancestors, sharing the fun with them as best you can.

- You could make an offering of roses to Astghik to symbolize how we remember and honor women whose power and importance may have been diminished.

Ghost Festival

THE FIFTEENTH DAY OF THE SEVENTH MONTH IN
THE LUNAR CALENDAR, USUALLY IN MID-JULY

The Ghost Festival is a traditional Taoist and Buddhist festival, which takes place for an entire month. Like Samhain and Día de Muertos, it is a time when ghosts and spirits, particularly those of our ancestors, can walk among us.

The Ghost Festival originates from an ancient Indian sutra that tells the story of Maudgalyayana, a close disciple of Buddha. When Maudgalyayana achieved abhijñā (higher knowledge, though not quite enlighten-ment), he used his new power to contact his deceased mother. But when he found her, she had been reborn into the ghost realm and was starving. Maudgalyayana tried to offer her a bowl of rice, but she could not eat it—the rice transformed into a burning coal instead. Buddha told Maudga-lyayana that he could only help his mother by offering food to monks at the end of the monsoon season (usually mid-July), who would then trans-fer it to the ghost realm.

Since then, however, the understanding of this tale has shifted—now, those in the ghost realm are able to venture into our reality at this time with more direct contact. It is believed that the ghosts who wander were not adequately honored at the time of their death and have long, thin necks, because they have been starved by their families. Family members will burn incense, offer food, and craft papier-mâché representations of various goods in the hopes of assisting their ancestors. Even if they don't know the ghosts or are not related to them, people will pay tribute to these lost souls, hoping to bring them peace so they do not intrude on the lives of the living. Monks and priests often throw rice, scattering it in the air and giving it to the ghosts who stand unseen beside us.

At the end of the festival, lotus-shaped lanterns are lit and cast out into the river and onto the sea, guiding these lost souls back to where they belong and can be at peace. When the lights go out, the ghosts have found their way home.

Bon or Obon is a Japanese festival that evolved from the same root celebration as the Ghost Festival. It has become something of a family reunion, when people return to their ancestral homes, leaving offerings and cleaning graves, but also enjoying the presence of family members they haven't seen in a long time. Families will light paper lanterns in their homes, calling to their ancestors to come visit.

Bon features a Bon Odori, or Bon dance, which is inspired by the same Buddhist story of Maudgalyayana. In this variation, when Maudgalyayana learned how he could help his deceased mother, he danced with joy. This dance can look different depending on where you are, as each region has its own style. However, a typical Bon dance takes place around a high wooden scaffold called a yagura, built especially for this festival. The musicians and singers perform from atop the yagura, while the dancers perform below, circling the structure.

At the end of the three-day festival, the families will send their ancestors back whence they came. The city of Kyoto lights five giant bonfires at different locations to help them find their way. At dusk, families also light toro nagashi, large paper lanterns that are cast afloat in the river, often crowding together into one large raft of light. When they burn out, the spirits are returned to the water.

WAYS TO CELEBRATE

◆ Leave offerings for your ancestors, and perhaps enjoy the thought that they might be nearby. Speak with them, even if it is only in your imagination.

◆ Consider how you can help lost souls—including those who are still with us. Perhaps make a donation of food or clothing to a homeless shelter.

◆ Light a lantern and send it down a stream, as a guide for any spirits who may need your assistance.

Lughnasadh

AUGUST 1–2

Lughnasadh is a Celtic/Gaelic festival that marks the beginning of harvest season. It occurs when we are finally able to reap the benefits of all our hard work planting, growing, and tending—right at the halfway point between the summer solstice (Litha) and the autumn equinox (Mabon).

It is named for the god Lugh, who was a member of the Tuatha Dé Danann, or fairy-gods. Lugh was a warrior, artisan, and natural leader, though Lughnasadh is observed less in honor of him and more in celebration and gratitude for his foster mother Tailtiu, who cleared the plains

of Ireland to ready them for planting before dying of exhaustion. Lugh created the holiday to honor her work and sacrifice, establishing a kind of Olympic Games called the áenach Tailteann on this day. All the warring factions of Ireland called a truce to attend these games, and there was horse racing, athletic contests, trading, music, storytelling, and, of course, matchmaking. Lughnasadh was second only to Beltane for its number of weddings.

Some of these weddings were only temporary, however, for a handfasting held at Tailteann could be a trial run, lasting only a year and a day. If at that time the couple wished for the marriage to be dissolved, they could stand on separate hills and go their separate ways.

As with Midsummer celebrations, the pagan traditions of Lughnasadh were incorporated into Christianity, under which umbrella the day is known as Lammas, or Loaf-Mass. It still marks the first fruits of the harvest, and parishioners bring a loaf made from the new crop into the church as an offering of thanks.

WAYS TO CELEBRATE

◆ Bake a loaf of bread as an offering to whomever you choose, with gratitude for the bounty of the harvest.

◆ Host some games in honor of Tailtiu! It doesn't have to be anything fancy—you could get friends together for a game of touch football or a pickup game of basketball.

◆ Consider Lughnasadh as a time to think on the permanence of your relationships. Do you need to stand on opposite hills with anyone?

FALL

THERE IS A LOT OF DIVERSITY WITHIN FALL RITUALS, PARTLY because there are so very many of them. While at first this may seem unusual, when we consider the many similarities in the various rituals we've seen for spring and summer, it does make a certain amount of sense. Fall represents the harvest, as well as the end of the rainy season in much of the world—which certainly calls for a party.

And yet, autumn is also the winding down of the year, when all that bloomed is beginning to fade. So it is also a time when people around the world think about their own fading and the winding down of life that comes to us all. These celebrations are about family and ancestral connection, but they are also about death in general. In spite of that, there is nothing somber or morbid in these holidays—they are instead a way of delighting in the dark and finding the joy, fun, and magic in even the most challenging times. When fall rolls around, we are beginning the process of letting go of the year, but we are also holding tight to the things that mean the most to us— the people we love and cherish. And we do this by sharing our lives with them, even the ones that are no longer living—and that is one of the most magical experiences we can ever know.

ANCESTRAL ALTAR

We may not always feel close to our families or know *how* to feel connected with them. Since so much of fall is about celebrating and tending to that connection, this ritual is a possible path toward strengthening that link. And if, on the other hand, you feel that connection already and have an amazing relationship with your family, that's great! This ritual will only serve to boost and further what is already established.

Choose a place for your altar. It can be quite small or as large as you want it to be, but make sure you've set aside a sacred space. Then gather the following items:

◆ **A CENTRAL IMAGE OR SYMBOL.** You can choose a picture of a particular ancestor—someone you admire or feel close to—or of a group of family members. You can choose an item that belonged to them or that represents your family in some way. You can opt for a piece of art that represents family in general. Listen to your intuition, and know that nothing is set in stone.

◆ **ELEMENTS.** Set the energetic boundaries of your altar by incorporating the elements of air, earth, fire, and water. You can use a feather, a rock, a candle or some incense, and a jar or bowl of water. Or you can use crystals that resonate with each of the elements:

Air.
Fluorite,
celestite,
amethyst

Earth.
Agate,
tigereye,
obsidian

Fire.
Carnelian,
citrine,
sunstone

Water.
Aquamarine,
opal,
moonstone

◆ **OFFERINGS.** The best way to feel connected to your ancestors is by intentionally leaving offerings. These can include apples, found objects like coins or pebbles, or foods you know they liked—whatever feels right. If you leave food, you'll want to remove it before it goes bad, knowing that the energy of the offering is all that's needed. If the food is still good, you should absolutely eat it if you want to! If you don't want to, just dispose of it respectfully. Refresh your offerings once a month or as often as you like.

MOON MEDITATION

The moon is a powerful source of magic all year round, but it feels particularly dynamic in the fall. This ritual is oriented around the Harvest Moon, the full moon in September, nearest the equinox.

On the day before the night of the full moon, gather leaves that have fallen. It's fairly early in the season, so depending on where you live, there may not be many but you can always find some. Look for a variety—crispy leaves, greenish leaves, and colorful leaves in all kinds of shapes and sizes.

As the moon rises, use your leaves to create a sacred circle around you. If you can do this outside, great, but indoors is fine, too. Close your eyes and breathe deeply, imagining a beam of energy tethering you to the rising moon. Feel its gravitational pull on you, helping you to sit up straighter with more energy. Imagine your heart rising with the moon as you breathe in and grounding down into the earth as you breathe out. Consider how day and night are equal—or close to equal—on this night. How can you find the balance between the two within yourself?

Continue to breathe in your sacred circle for as long as you like, feeling the blessings of the moon, the earth, and the leaves you have collected and the support Mother Nature has to give you.

Homowo

MID-AUGUST

Homowo translates from the Ga language to "hoot-at-hunger" and commemorates a famine that took place in Ghana hundreds of years ago. The Ga people of Ghana represent around 10 percent of the population there, and during this time they celebrate their survival of the drought that nearly destroyed their tribe.

Homowo takes place over several months, beginning in May when the millet is sowed and the fishing season begins. Then in June, after the crops are planted, a silence falls over the community. It is believed that too much noise will harm the crops and scare away the ancestors. For the month, there is a ban on drumming, and bars and nightclubs remain closed.

After that, Ga people who are living elsewhere in the world come home to visit their families. Their arrival usually happens on a Thursday

in August, and so they are known as Soobii, the Thursday people. This day marks the beginning of a time of peace and harmony, as all family arguments are set aside, and sometimes even forgiven.

On Friday, twins and triplets are honored as signs of great fertility in a nod to the population loss during the famine. That night, there is often gunfire in the streets, marking the end of the ban on drumming and warning everyone to stay inside, as the spirits are definitely out and about now.

On Saturday, Homowo Day, there is a feast, and everyone brings food from their harvests to prepare a dinner for both the living and the dead. They eat fish, palm soup, and kpokpoi—a dish made of steamed and fermented cornmeal and palm oil. Priests will wander the feasts and sprinkle kpokpoi around to feed the ancestors.

After the feast, there is parade, beginning with the priests drumming on their knees. Then everyone joins in, with drums and dancing, mocking hunger in their triumph over it and feeling gratitude for the gods.

WAYS TO CELEBRATE

◆ The tradition of forgiveness on Homowo is such an important one. We all struggle with our families, and setting aside a time to let go of and forget those struggles allows us to maintain the relationships that are most important to us, even when things get hard.

◆ Have a feast! Invite your family over for a meal, both the living and the dead, and feel grateful for all you have.

◆ You may also want to hoot at hunger in your own way by donating to a local food bank, making a donation to a part of the world that is in need, or volunteering at a soup kitchen.

Gai Jatra

THE FIRST DAY OF THE DARK FORTNIGHT OF THE MONTH OF GUNLA IN
THE NEPALESE CALENDAR; USUALLY THE FIFTEENTH DAY OF THE EIGHTH
LUNAR MONTH, USUALLY AUGUST OR SEPTEMBER

The Cow Festival celebrated in Nepal dates back to Pratap Malla, king
of Kathmandu in the mid-1600s. Pratap Malla and his wife had lost their
young son, and the queen was distraught. Nothing could relieve her grief,
and in his desperation, Pratap Malla held a parade. He asked every family who had lost a loved one that year to show the queen that she was not

alone—and, if they could, to make her smile. The people came out in costumes, dancing and cavorting, and eventually the queen did smile.

Since then it has been tradition for all who have lost someone to lead a young cow along the streets so that the cow may guide their loved one to the gates of heaven. According to some beliefs, on this day souls can enter the world of the dead without having to go through multiple reincarnations. In times when people could not afford a cow, young children would be dressed as cows and led playfully in the calf's place. There are still costumes, and general merrymaking abounds.

Gai Jatra serves as a reminder that death visits us all and we will all lose someone to it. We will experience grief and sorrow, but we must still smile again.

WAYS TO CELEBRATE

- As much as we try to avoid thinking about it, we will all die someday. Is it possible to hold that knowledge and still laugh? Perhaps consider journaling about how to do that.

- Tell funny stories about any loved ones you have lost in the past year.

- Do something kind for someone who is hurting—try to make them smile.

Moon Festival

THE FIFTEENTH DAY OF THE EIGHTH LUNAR MONTH,
USUALLY MID-SEPTEMBER

The Moon Festival falls on the night of the full moon during the eighth month of the Chinese calendar—it is believed to be the night when the moon shines at its brightest and most full. This midautumn festival dates back over 3,000 years and is held in celebration of Chang'e, the Chinese moon goddess. Similar festivals occur across Asia—known as Chuseok in Korea, Tsukimi in Japan, and Tet Trung Thu in Vietnam.

In ancient China, the moon and water were deeply intertwined with the concepts of rejuvenation and fertility—as the moon grows in size

throughout the lunar cycle, she is pregnant, and she gives birth at the final crescent before the new moon.

There are several legends around Chang'e, but the one most often told during the Moon Festival centers around rejuvenation. Chang'e, a mortal woman, was married to Hou Yi, a famous archer. At this time, there were ten suns, and they all rose in the sky at the same time, wreaking havoc with the earth and harvest. Hou Yi shot down nine of the suns, leaving us with just one, which is all we truly need. The goddess Xiwangmu was impressed and gave him an elixir of life to grant him immortality. But Hou Yi did not want to live forever without Chang'e, so he put the elixir aside.

Chang'e was tempted by it, though, and one night she drank the elixir herself. As she did, she drifted up into the night sky and became the moon. Hou Yi was understandably hurt and angered by this, and shot arrow after arrow at her, but he missed every time—perhaps he didn't truly want to harm her. As the months went by, Hou Yi missed his wife and gazed up at her. He began to leave offerings of cakes to the woman he loved, who had become the goddess of the moon.

Since then, offerings have been left for Chang'e, and it is believed that she grants wishes, usually ones about children and fertility. Moon cakes unlikely were her favorite dessert, since they appeared many years later, but the favorite food of the Moon Festival is this cake—a round pastry filled with a thick, usually sweet paste.

These days, like many rituals in Chinese culture, the Moon Festival centers around family, with everyone coming together and enjoying one another. It is a night filled with gratitude for the coming harvest, and it is lit with lanterns.

WAYS TO CELEBRATE

◆ Look for the face of Chang'e in the full moon, and ask her to grant a wish.

◆ Purchase moon cakes—or make your own!—and share them with family, slicing them into pie shapes and enjoying them with tea.

◆ Invite family members over for dinner, and gather outside in the evening to enjoy the moonlight together.

Mabon

THE FALL EQUINOX

Fall equinox celebrations serve as a kind of second harvest, when the colder air is producing carrots, other root vegetables, and most importantly, apples. This holiday is referred to as Mabon in witchy circles, but that name was only coined in the 1970s with the resurgence of Wicca. The day was named for a Welsh god, the son of the earth goddess Modron. When he was three nights old, he was stolen from her arms and taken to the underworld, and it would be many years before he was rescued by Arthur and returned to the light.

Sound familiar? The fall equinox was also when Persephone jour-neyed to Hades each year, to return at Ostara to her mother Demeter. It's yet another spin on the story of the Oak King and the Holly King—more folklore of the shifting seasons.

Like the spring equinox, the hours of sunlight are equal to the hours of darkness on Mabon—but we know that from this point on, it's just going to get darker and darker. Mabon is about acknowledging and accepting that darkness. So many of our rituals around the world celebrate the sun; there are only a few that celebrate the night, and Mabon is one of them. But unlike Samhain or Día de Muertos or the Ghost Festival, Mabon isn't about death—it's about life.

We often associate darkness with death, but half of our lives are spent in darkness. That darkness is a gift in itself. It is a time to rest, and to think. And so Mabon is a somewhat subdued celebration—there is feasting, yes, because there is always feasting—but there is also quiet reflection, time spent looking at our own darkness, our own faults and flaws, so that we may begin to release them. And there is gratitude, for all that we receive.

WAYS TO CELEBRATE

◆ Write a gratitude list, including the things you hadn't necessarily considered being thankful for in the past.

◆ Light a bonfire and roast some apples in the coals.

◆ Write down something you want to release—some darkness within yourself that you want to bring into the light—and throw it into the bonfire or burn it with a candle.

Sukkot

BEGINNING THE FIFTEENTH DAY OF THE JEWISH MONTH
OF TISHREI, USUALLY SEPTEMBER OR OCTOBER

Sukkot begins five days after Yom Kippur, the Jewish day of atonement, and it lasts for seven days. It is named for sukkah, little huts built by hand in the days preceding the holiday. Sukkah have at least three sides and a thatched roof and are meant to represent the huts the Israelites dwelt in during their forty years of wandering the desert after escaping slavery in Egypt. But much of Sukkot also focuses on the harvest and thanking God for all we have received this year.

For all seven days, families will eat and sometimes even sleep in the sukkah, and this enforced simplicity and rustic living helps take them out of their routine, giving them time to consider what is truly important. On the first day, in a ritual called ushpizin, ancestors are invited to partake in the meal. Each day of the holiday there is also a taking of the "Four Kinds"—a collection of symbolic plants, including citron, called strong; a palm frond, called Lulu; three myrtle twigs, called hadassim; and two willow twigs, called aravot. After a blessing is recited, the Four Kinds are brought together and waved in all six directions—right, left, forward, up, down, and behind. According to rabbinic lore, the Four Kinds represent the various personalities that make up the community of Israel and acknowledge that they must all come together in order to create a harmonious whole.

WAYS TO CELEBRATE

◆ Spend a night or two camping, either in a cabin or tent, to take you away from your routine and allow for some thoughtfulness around what you truly need to be happy.

◆ Consider the disparate personalities in your family and community and how they all differ from and support one another.

◆ Gather some type of "Four Kinds" that works for you, using plants that grow where you live, to symbolize a coming together.

Bathukamma

BEGINNING IN THE LATTER HALF OF MONSOON SEASON, BEFORE THE
ONSET OF WINTER, USUALLY SEPTEMBER OR OCTOBER

This festival of flowers represents the cultural spirit of the Telangana region of India. It is observed in honor of Gauri, the Hindu goddess of fertility, motherhood, marriage, and devotion, and as such it honors and celebrates all women.

Bathukamma is a nine-day ritual, though the first several days are spent in preparation. Women clean the home, then place cow dung cakes around the house to welcome Gauri and ask for her blessings. The men of the house go out into the plains to gather flowers, for after the monsoons have passed, the fields are bright with color. The women sort the flowers by size and color, and then arrange them into intricate cones.

On the final day, the women dress in sari and jewels, while teenaged girls wear a traditional half-sari called a langa oni and dance around the Bathukamma arrangements, singing folk songs. They are joined by the women in a circle of unity and femininity. At last, the cones are set to float in the river or immersed in a pond, and a handmade mud figure of Gauri is immersed, releasing her back into the river or pond to feed and tend to it. The figure is decorated with turmeric, and as it dissolves, the women anoint each other with its golden paste.

This festival is inspired by a number of myths. One holds that Gauri killed the demon Mahishasura and then, exhausted, slept until her devotees woke her with their prayers. Another tells the story of a king and queen who had lost one hundred sons to war and prayed for Lakshmi to be reborn in their home—which she agreed to do. In either version, the contribution of women is honored, highlighting both their strength and their peaceful natures.

WAYS TO CELEBRATE

- Gather flowers! In much of the United States, these will likely be among the last blooms of the year, so it's a wonderful opportunity to go out into nature and gather some blossoms. Get creative and design an intricate floral arrangement.

- Get dressed up and spend a day honoring femininity in all its forms.

- Celebrate sisterhood by getting together with the women in your life—your friends, your mother, your sisters. Feel how powerful you are together.

Diwali

THE FULL MOON DURING THE MONTH OF KARTIKA IN THE
HINDU CALENDAR, OCTOBER OR NOVEMBER

Diwali is a complex five-day festival celebrated by Hindus, Jains, Sikhs, and Newar Buddhists. There are a variety of different meanings and rituals associated with it—according to one tradition, Diwali is the day Rama reached the city of Ayodhya and defeated the demon king Ravana. In another, it is the day after Krishna, an avatar of Vishnu, killed the demon Narakasura. Regardless of the specifics, the general theme of this Festival of Lights is the triumph of light over darkness, good over evil, and knowledge over ignorance.

◆ **THE FIRST DAY** of Diwali, known as Dhanteras, is a time for Hindus to clean their homes and set up diyas, small oil-filled lamps that will remain lit for the next five days to honor Lakshmi, the goddess of wealth and prosperity, and Ganesha, the god of intellect and wisdom. The doorways are decorated with rangoli—intricate designs made from colored rice flour, sand, and flower petals. Lights and lanterns are strung up on the roofs and walls. It's a night for cleansing, renewal, and good health.

◆ **THE SECOND DAY** of Diwali, known as Naraka Chaturdashi, has a somewhat darker flavor, though it is still very much a celebration. Rituals on this day are focused on liberating the souls of any spirits that may be stuck, lighting the way to their reincarnation. The day is also spent in preparation, with people making sweets and treats to enjoy on the third day.

◆ **THE THIRD DAY** of Diwali, Lakshmi Pujan, is the height of the festival. Lakshmi, who is married to Lord Vishnu, will visit all her devotees on this night and bestow her blessings—and the more honored she is, the more she will give. Diya lights are placed in windowsills and on ledges to invite her into the home. It is believed that she will visit the cleanest house first, so this process is done very carefully and reverentially. The cleaning also echoes the end of monsoon season and the rinsing that the rain has given the earth.

At dusk, pujas, or rituals of worship, are performed in Lakshmi's honor. First, the space is cleansed by burning incense, and a cloth is laid on the altar. Then, celebrants sprinkle grains in the center of the cloth, and place a kalasha (a metal pitcher) on top. They will fill the kalasha with water, betel nuts, flowers, coins, and rice. Then, they will place a dish of rice atop the kalasha and draw a lotus on the rice using turmeric powder. Finally, they will place an idol of Lakshmi on top and surround it with coins. Ganesha is also honored during a puja, with his idol placed in front of the kalasha.

Once the setup is over, the worship can commence. Offerings of turmeric, kumkuma powder, and flowers are made to Lakshmi and placed in the water. Worshippers may also invoke Saraswati, goddess of knowledge, art, and wisdom. Lakshmi's idol is bathed with panchamrita, a sweet ritual libation, and then rinsed with ritual water. She is given more offerings, including flowers, saffron, perfume, and sweets, and her story, "Lakshmi Puran," is recited. The ritual is closed with Aarti, or the reverential passing of flame between all participants.

Mothers, who embody Lakshmi, are honored for their hard work on this day. After the puja, everyone ventures outside to light fireworks and celebrate, while at the same time driving away any evil spirits that might be lingering. After the fireworks, there is a feast, and everyone enjoys all the good food that was prepared the day before.

◆ THE FOURTH DAY of Diwali has a few names, including Govardhan Puja and Padwa. It is associated with a number of legends, including Vishnu's defeat of Bali, Parvati's defeat of her husband Shiva at a game of dyuta, and the day Krishna defeated Indra by lifting the Govardhan Mountain. Many communities use this day to celebrate the bond between husband and wife, and sometimes they also build a small hillock out of cow dung to represent the mountain. There is a mountain of food consumed, with up to a hundred different dishes on offer.

◆ **THE LAST DAY** of the festival is Bhaj Dooj, or Brother's Day. This may reference Yama and his sister Yamuna, or Krishna and his sister Subhadra, but either way, it is a time to celebrate the bond between brother and sister. Sisters perform a puja in honor of their brothers and feed them with their hands.

WAYS TO CELEBRATE

◆ The triumph of light over darkness, and of knowledge over ignorance, is always worth celebrating. Light some candles and tell stories of these victories, treasuring these legends, no matter the culture.

◆ The act of cleaning as preparation for coming prosperity is an inspiring way to make a chore into a ritual.

◆ Reach out to all the people in your life who are honored on Diwali—your mother, any husbands or wives, and any siblings. It's a good time to connect to the people who are most important to you.

Samhain

OCTOBER 31

There are Neolithic-era tombs in Ireland that are aligned with sunrise at the time of Samhain—and no wonder, for that is the day, in Celtic pagan culture, when the dead walk.

As on Beltane, the veil between worlds is thin and the fairies might come visiting along with the dead. And so the cattle were brought down from the hills, counted and slaughtered, and protective bonfires were lit. People would make offerings of food and drink to the fairies and the dead. These offerings were meant to appease any spirits that might be angry or vengeful, but plates were often laid out at the table for friendlier ancestors to come join in the feast.

Samhain was also a night for divination, often done using the ritual bonfires. Two hazelnuts roasted together could let intended couples know if they were going to be happy together—if the nuts jumped away from the heat, there was likely to be strife, but if they roasted gently side by side, it would be a good marriage. Coins, rings, and other trinkets were hidden in cakes; if you got the piece with the coin, you would prosper, and if you got the piece with the ring, a wedding would soon occur. Bobbing for apples—which we still do today!—was a kind of divination, as the teeth marks could be read.

The tradition of wearing costumes and trick-or-treating on Halloween dates back to this ritual. In order to hide from the fairies and spirits, people would dress with their clothes inside out, in white, or as other genders to confuse them.

Some people would dress as spirits or fairies themselves, to symbolically receive offerings and praise in their place. Of course, it isn't much of a leap to move from dressing as an unpredictable spirit to behaving like one, and soon enough Samhain became known as Mischief Night, with pranks being played and general mild mayhem abounding. But in the spirit of community happiness, "trick or treat" has become an empty threat, and Halloween can supply candy cupboards for the rest of the year.

WAYS TO CELEBRATE

- ◆ Set a place at your table for a deceased loved one, and leave food and drink outside for spirits that don't have a home to go to.

- ◆ Leave a candle in a western window to guide your ancestors home, and light a jack-o'-lantern to ward off the spirits you don't want to come calling.

- ◆ Go trick-or-treating! This most fun Halloween ritual is absolutely a way to celebrate Samhain.

Día de Muertos

NOVEMBER 1–2

Día de Muertos is a joyful celebration of death. If that feels like an oxymoron, it isn't, for on this day it is believed that the veil between worlds is thin and the dead can walk among us. Rather than working to send them back home, people in Mexico and around the world lovingly welcome them in, embracing this time together.

The celebration dates back to Aztec festivals that celebrated death. Back then, family members would often provide food, water, and tools to help their loved ones find their way to Chicunamictlán, the Land of the Dead. Since then, the culture has shifted to accommodate Spanish and other European influences, with figures of death portrayed by skeletons.

To welcome these deceased family members, people will build ofrendas, or altars dedicated specifically to them, with their favorite foods, photos, possessions, and more. They can be constructed in the home, at cemeteries, or in public spaces, and often feature papel picado, or elaborately cut paper, and cempasúchil, or marigolds, as the vibrant color is believed to attract the departed souls.

The graves are cleaned and decorated, and toys are left for dead children, while bottles of tequila or mezcal are left for dead adults. Afterward, family members and friends might sit around the ofrenda, telling stories of their deceased loved ones, laughing, and singing and dancing. They may also write and perform calaveras literarias, or short rhyming poems that celebrate/poke fun at the deceased, sort of like a poetic roast.

Sometimes the celebration will turn into a community-wide festival, with parades and enormous ofrendas, giant skeletons, and people wearing catrina, or skeleton face paint. They enjoy pan de muerto, a special sweet roll made for this day, and calaveras, or skulls made of sugar that have been decorated to reflect the personality of the person they are representing. It is believed that the spirits of the dead eat the essence of the foods left for them, so though the food is all much too good to throw away, when it is eaten after the festivities, it is believed to have no nutritional value. People will also drink pulque, a milky beverage made from fermented agave sap, or they will share the favorite beverages of their deceased ancestors.

WAYS TO CELEBRATE

◆ So many of the rituals in this book honor our ancestors, but Día de Muertos is the most fun—there is a laughter and joy in dealing with death that can be inspirational to those of us outside of this culture who more often fear and dread death. Consider having a laugh with your loved ones who have passed, telling funny stories about them, and feeling as if they are there with you.

◆ Consider writing a calaveras literarias.

◆ Make an ancestral altar of your own, inspired by ofrendas, as a way to keep your loved ones near and invite them into your home even after they've gone.

Loi Krathong

THE FULL MOON OF THE TWELFTH MONTH IN THE
THAI LUNAR CALENDAR, USUALLY NOVEMBER

Loi Krathong is a Thai ritual celebration of water, which marks the end of the rainy season. Krathong are small floating containers often made of a slice of a banana tree or a spider lily plant, though more modern ones can be made of bread. On this night, they are decorated and filled with three incense sticks and a candle, as well as a coin that serves as an offering to the river spirits. The krathong are launched into the river with a wish.

It is said that Loi Krathong began because of a legend starring a beautiful woman named Nang Nopphamat. She wanted to catch the eye of the king, and so she crafted a lotus-shaped float and sent it downriver. It worked, and nowadays there are beauty contests to determine who will be this year's Nopphamat Queen.

The krathong can also symbolize letting go. Sometimes people even place a lock of hair into the krathong to represent that release of whatever they no longer want to carry. People may pray to Phra Mae Khongkha, the Thai goddess of the waters, who is related to the Hindu river goddess Ganga. They give thanks for her life-giving gifts, and ask her forgiveness when they have polluted her waters.

There is another festival, Yi Peng, that is celebrated in Thailand at the same time as Loi Krathong, though it has more Buddhist overtones. On Yi Peng, instead of sending lights downriver, gorgeous and often quite large paper lanterns known as khom loi are sent into the air. They are made of a light material, usually rice paper, with a candle at their center. The heat from the fire puffs up the lantern until eventually it lifts off. Thousands of lanterns float through the night sky, releasing any mistakes or bad luck into the darkness. If your lantern stays lit so long that you can no longer find it amid the others, you will have good luck in the next year.

The Cambodian Water Festival is similar to both the Moon Festival and Loi Krathong, but it has its own flavor and lore. Occurring at the end of monsoon season, it begins when the flow of the Tonle Sap River reverses, moving to the conjunction or chaktomuk, which is where three rivers—the Mekong, the Bassac, and the Tonle Sap—all come together into a single body of water.

The Cambodian goddess Preah Mae Kongkea is derived from Ganga, but she has a much wider purview. She is the mother of all earthly water, including seas, rivers, and lakes, which provide all that is necessary for her people to live on. During the first day of the festival, people pray to her at the Tonle Sap River, offering their thanks.

The second day is dedicated to the moon, but it is a much more fun and less mysterious celebration than most lunar rituals. At twelve minutes past midnight, lanterns are lit in honor of the Moon Rabbit, who offered himself as food to Sàkra, the ruler of heaven, when he was disguised as an old man. Sàkra then placed his likeness on the moon, so that all would remember his generosity. After the lanterns are lit, celebrants enjoy bananas or coconut syrup with ambok, a traditional flattened rice dish.

The festival also includes a boat race to commemorate the victory of the Khmer navy in 1181. The race includes a female dancer who perches on the bow of the boat, representing the boat's spirit. There are eyes painted on the prow of the boat, and dozens of paddlers work in unison to cross the finish line.

WAYS TO CELEBRATE

◆ Cast a small handmade boat out into the water, floating a candle in it. You can place a lock of hair inside and send your negative thoughts away with it.

◆ Give thanks to the earth or whatever deity is appropriate for you, in gratitude for water and all that it does for us.

◆ Look for the rabbit in the moon.

Makahiki

BEGINS THE NIGHT MAKALI'I CONSTELLATION (PLEIADES) RISES OVER
PU'U O MAHUKA HEIAU, USUALLY MID-NOVEMBER

The Hawaiian celebration of Makahiki begins in November and lasts into early spring. The Hawaiian calendar recognizes two seasons: Makahiki, the time of harvest and rest, and the remaining eight months, the time of labor, agriculture, and war. Conflict and work of any kind was prohibited during the months of Makahiki, and the Kanaka Maoli (Hawaiian people) instead made offerings to Lono, the god of fertility, agriculture, music, peace, and rainfall.

Being so close to the equator, Hawaii doesn't experience seasons the way much of the world does—but there is a rainy season, and it begins with Makahiki. Lono brings the rains to the leeward parts of the islands—those that are usually dry—and allows the hard work of the rest of the year to bear fruit. While his rains do their work, there is feasting and celebration, often in the form of competitive games, like a kind of Olympics.

After offerings were made to Lono at heiau (temples) and ahu (altars), an image of the god was brought clockwise around the island so that each community could pay their respects and receive his blessing. Once he completed his journey, the games could begin. There was hula, pahe'e (javelin-throwing), ulu maika (a form of lawn bowling), and he'e hōlua, or sled-riding. The sled was formed much like a flexible flyer, but instead of riding over snow a course was built of rock and grass, and competitors would often ride their sleds standing, as a kind of land-surfing.

Toward the end of Makahiki season, a special canoe called the wa'a 'auhau was loaded with ho'okupu (offerings) and set adrift at sea as a gift of thanks to Lono. Today, Makahiki celebrations occur in schools in Hawaii as an extended field day, and many cultural practitioners still make their offerings and even ride the hōlua on ancient courses that remain.

WAYS TO CELEBRATE

- An extended period of rest is unlikely to be available to you—though wouldn't it be nice if it were?—but this might be a good time to take a vacation. The year is winding down. Take a few days to play and relax and enjoy the company of the people you care about.

- Make some offerings to show your appreciation for the rain and the growing season.

- Play some outdoor games, if you can! In the Northern Hemisphere, the weather is likely to get unpleasant soon. Take advantage of the crisp air and run around outside!

WINTER

THE WILDEST CELEBRATIONS OF THE YEAR TEND TO FALL IN winter. This might seem surprising at first, given how we all tend to hunker down in the cold. But then again doesn't everyone go a little stir-crazy after too much time indoors?

There is also a sense of urgency, a need to contribute our own bit of energy, passion, and, yes, chaos, as a way to cajole the sun to return and bring us back its warmth and life.

Winter celebrations are a triumph of light, of staying up late with rituals of playful misrule. There is gratitude and planning for the coming warmth, releasing all that the previous year held, welcoming in the new. When winter arrives, hold close all that you hold dear—whether that includes the people you love, the cozy activities that bring you joy, or the values that have informed the way you have lived the year thus far. Use your love to cast a blessing over all of these, shining your warmth and energy on all that is most important to you.

CANDLE SPELL

Winter is a time to celebrate light in the darkness, and what better way to do that than with a candle? This spell is best performed at night in a darkened room. You'll want to have enough light so you can see, but you also want it to be dark enough so that your candle casts a circle of light, flickering and dancing in the dark.

Choose your candle—it can be tapered, scented, in a jar, whatever you like. Listen to your intuition and feel what is right for your spell, today. What are you hoping to set alight?

Anoint the sides of your candle with essential oils:

◆

**LAVENDER,
FRANKINCENSE,
OR MYRRH**
for intuition, for
seeing in the dark

◆

THYME OR MINT
for clarity

◆

**GINGER, LEMON, OR
SWEET ORANGE**
for brightness
and energy

Light your candle right at the moment the sun goes down, serving as your own light in the darkness and allowing the flame to maintain a connection with the sun, even when we cannot see it. If you like, take a slip of paper and write down your intentions for this light or a phrase that symbolizes the light within you that you wish to bring forth. It can even be as simple as just the one word: *light*. Set the paper on fire with the flame of the candle and let it drop onto a plate, releasing the energy of your spell into the night.

CHAOS MAGIC

We should all embrace the spirit of winter's celebration of misrule. The intention behind chaos magic is really all that matters, as the entire system requires *not* having a system in the first place. Instead, you must simply trust your instincts and intuition, using your personal power to work your magic however you see fit. That said, a little guidance can be helpful if you're relatively new to the practice, so here is a framework for you to create your own joyful misrule:

- ◆ Rearrange the furniture in your house. You don't have to leave it like that and you don't have to shift everything, but try upending the structure of your home just to see how it shifts your perspective.

◆ Create some art, actively working to make it nonrepresenta-
tional. Abstract art is emotional, intuitive, and magical. Explore!

◆ Try out "cut-up magic." Write down a poem or some song lyrics
or a sentence someone said to you—it can be anything—and
then cut it up randomly, slicing out words, phrases, and even
parts of words. Scatter the bits of paper and arrange them in
new ways, drawing a fresh meaning out of them.

◆ Create a sigil by writing down a phrase that represents something you want to embody or something you feel gratitude for,
like "I bring light and joy to the darkness" or "I am blessed by
the light and the darkness." Remove all but the first letters of
the most important words, so "IBLJD" or "IBLD." Next, craft
your letters into an artistic symbol, obscuring the letters and
making them into something beautiful. Bury your sigil outdoors, nourishing the earth with your magic.

Soyal

THE WINTER SOLSTICE

The Pueblo, Zuni, and Hopi peoples mark the winter solstice as the beginning of the second phase of creation. They welcome the kachinas, or spirit messengers, as they bring the sun back from its slumber. Soyal is a ritual celebration that works to pull the sun forth, bringing it onto the path of

warmth and growth. It is believed that everything that will occur in the year to come is arranged during Soyal.

In the days and weeks before the event, people prepare by making prayer sticks of feathers and piñon needles called pahos. Children are taught about the kachinas and are given intricately carved statuettes that represent some of the hundreds of distinct kachina spirits.

What happens during the actual Soyal ceremonies is kept private by the individual tribes. Generally, though, they involve dancing, often with the kachinas, as a way to invoke the sun and life. People will also descend into a kiva—a ceremonial chamber that is partially underground—and stomp on the sipapu, a symbolic hole covered by a board, meant to represent the entrance to the underworld—the place where the sun has been held back and now needs to be broken free.

At the end of the ceremony, the kachinas will remain with the people for the first half of the year, returning to their homes in the mountains at the summer solstice, in a ritual celebration called Niman.

WAYS TO CELEBRATE

- ◆ Welcoming the sun back to the world is something that can be done in a variety of ways—and dancing is certainly one of them!

- ◆ You could do some winter cleaning outdoors, preparing the earth for the warmth that is yet to come.

- ◆ Consider how your own light may have been metaphorically blocked. How can you release it?

Yaldā

THE WINTER SOLSTICE

This Persian celebration, also known as Chelleh, dates back to at least the tenth century. It was believed that daevas, or Zoroastrian supernatural entities with potential malicious intent, would roam this night in service of Angra Mainyu, the spiritual embodiment of evil. People would remain awake all night, keeping watch with family and friends, finding safety in numbers, and sharing the last remaining fruit of the year, which was stored up for this occasion. On the next morning, all would celebrate having survived the night.

Today, there is less fear and more joy in rituals of Yaldā. People do stay awake late into the night—often all night—and they do gather together with family and friends. They share fruit, including watermelon and pomegranate, with their red and yellow glow symbolizing the sun and life. Eating watermelons is said to ensure health and well-being in the coming summer, keeping everyone from overheating. Some believe that eating carrots, pears, pomegranates, and green olives will protect from insect bites, particularly scorpions, and garlic will keep joints healthy.

After dinner, the elders of the family will tell stories, often reading from the Divān Hāfez, a collection of poetry that is used for divination. But only the first three volunteers will receive readings—for after that, it is said that Hāfez will be angry.

WAYS TO CELEBRATE

- Share some fruit, including watermelon, to welcome the sun and to shore up some protection against its heat in the coming summer.

- Stay up late, or even all night, with family and friends, telling stories and keeping each other lighthearted in the dark.

- Read some poetry, perhaps for divination, or perhaps just for the pleasure in the rhythm and magic of the words.

Dongzhi

THE WINTER SOLSTICE

This traditional Chinese holiday dates back to 206 BCE and is celebrated throughout East Asia. *Dongzhi* translates to "the extreme of winter"—and while the weather may get colder in the days to come, this longest night is indeed winter darkness at its most extreme. We can think of Dongzhi as the height of yin, as well. After this day the pendulum will begin to swing back toward yang and the balance between the two.

Like many festivals, Dongzhi once centered around the harvest, but today it has become more focused on family. There are a wide variety of traditional foods for this night, and many of them revolve around rice, including rice cakes, rice porridge, and tangyuan, which are glutinous balls of rice in a sweet broth.

In northern China, however, it is traditional to eat dumplings. The story goes that Zhang Zhongjing, a physician in the Han dynasty, saw people suffering from chilblains on their ears and ordered his apprentices to make ear-shaped dumplings with lamb in broth and distribute them. Since then people have always eaten dumplings to keep warm on Dongzhi.

In Taiwan, Dongzhi is taken particularly seriously, since in Taiwanese culture, winter is a time of rest and hibernation, when the body should be nourished. People make nine-layer cakes with glutinous rice flour; each layer is made in the shape of an auspicious animal, including a chicken, duck, tortoise, pig, cow, and sheep.

In South Korea, the traditional foods include a red bean porridge called patjuk, as red is a lucky color. People exchange gifts of calendars and socks and hope for snow—as a snow-filled winter is likely to bring a good harvest.

WAYS TO CELEBRATE

- Hoping for snow is traditional just about everywhere. Whether or not it genuinely brings a good harvest and whether or not we will enjoy a heavy snowfall once it comes, it always feels wonderful to have snow on the solstice. If it does snow, go out and play in it, and then come in and eat some nourishing broth with dumplings.

- Taking inspiration from the animal world and hibernating for a bit is an excellent idea. Bundle up for a day or two—or longer, if you can—and stay indoors, keeping cozy and resting.

- Consider how yin or feminine energy might be at its most extreme on the solstice. How can you embody and celebrate that?

Inti Raymi

THE WINTER SOLSTICE IN THE SOUTHERN HEMISPHERE

Inti Raymi is an Incan festival that dates back to 1412, when it was created by Sapa Inca Pachacuti, the ninth Incan emperor, to honor the sun god Inti. This celebration marked the beginning of the Incan new year and symbolized the mythical origin of the Incan people. It lasted for nine days, centering around the winter solstice, and took place in the plaza of the city of Huakaypata, or what is now Cusco.

Three days before the start of the festival, celebrants—which included members of the army, the nobility, and the Sapa Inca himself—would purify

themselves by fasting. Then, on the solstice, the Sapa Inca would step onto a platform and drink chicha de jora, a ceremonial beverage made of maize. Inside the Corichanca, the temple of the sun, a priest would light a flame to invoke Inti. The watching crowd would sing and dance.

And then there would be ritual sacrifices—most times of four black llamas, which would be cut open with a tumi, or ceremonial knife, so their entrails could be examined by priests to determine what the coming year would be like. But according to chronicler Juan de Betanzos, in lean years children under ten would be sacrificed, as well. The offerings were meant to please Inti when he was farthest away and beseech him to return to give life to the land.

In 1572, the Spanish conquistadores and their Catholic priests banned Inti Raymi celebrations. They did carry on in secret in more rural villages, but the Sapa Inca was no longer allowed to participate. Instead, this festival of the sun merged with the feast day of St. John the Baptist, and so became a Christian ceremony.

In 1944, Faustino Espinoza Navarro, a Peruvian writer and actor, revived Inti Raymi. It became a theatrical performance, and today up to 700 people participate. Navarro played the Sapa Inca for the first twelve years, and then handed the role off to a chosen successor. Today, the roles of the Sapa Inca and his wife are the most coveted. Thousands of people from all over the world come to watch the colorful and musical ritual performance. At dawn, the actors gather at Coricancha, and the Sapa Inca addresses the rising sun. Then they march in a procession through Cusco to the ruins of Sacsayhuaman, Pachacuti's palace. At exactly 1:30 p.m., the Sapa Inca drinks the ritual chicha, and offers a glass to Inti. There is a staged llama sacrifice, but no animals are harmed. There are dances and more performances, representing each of the four regions of Pachacuti's ancient empire.

WAYS TO CELEBRATE

◆ Making an offering to the sun is a way to express gratitude for the world in which we live—the miracle of life on a planet circling just the right distance from a star. That can be a glass of beer or whiskey, a citrus fruit, or any kind of created art. It's up to you!

◆ Find the moment on the solstice when the sun is highest in the sky, directly overhead, and welcome it home. Look up at it, and let its warmth land on your face.

◆ Sacrifices do not have to be bloody. What is something you can give up to show your appreciation and urge the sun to return?

Yule

THE WINTER SOLSTICE

Like Midsummer, Yule is a widespread European ritual celebration with Germanic, Gaelic, and druidic influences. In this case, it has remained fairly separate from Christianity, though several Yuletide rituals have been incorporated into traditional Christmas rituals. Documentation of Yule celebrations date back to the fourth century. As with other festivals of the sun around the world, there are several archaeological locations that were built in alignment with this celestial body. One such is Newgrange in Ireland—a passage tomb built in 3200 BCE, well before Stonehenge or the Egyptian pyramids. On the winter solstice, a small skylight above the entrance fills with light, which extends through the chamber, illuminating the passageway.

Some Yule rituals in Iceland and other Nordic countries are dedicated to Odin and Freya—and it is on this longest night that Odin leads a hunt across the sky. Interestingly, Celtic folklore holds that a similar Wild Hunt takes place on this night, but it is led by Fionn MacCool, an Irish folk hero. And in Wales, the Wild Hunt is led by Arawn, the god of the underworld. In some pagan and Wiccan traditions, it is led by the Horned God.

No matter the case, it is on this night that the Holly King is at the height of his power, though it will begin to wane with the dawn. We may be tempted to view the Holly King as evil, since he is dark and cold, but consider as well that holly bears magical, protective powers. We plant it near our homes or as a hedge so that its thorny leaves will keep out invaders, both physical and energetic.

The old song "The Holly and The Ivy" is no Christmas carol, but a wassail, which is a traditional song sung on Yule. Like holly, ivy is an evergreen: a plant that lives on through the long, cold dark as a reminder that life also continues through the dark—and that, in fact, darkness is a part of life.

And then there's mistletoe. More than a narrative device used in romantic comedies, mistletoe is part of an ancient Nordic tradition of peace on Yule. If warriors met in the forest beneath mistletoe, they were obliged to lay down their arms—and so, mistletoe was brought indoors for Yuletide to foster peace beneath it. Since then, the notion of peace has evolved to be a bit more romantic, which is certainly good fun. As it happens, mistletoe is a bit of a botanical parasite, eating away at its host tree, which is often the oak. Because of this, on or around Yule, druidic elders would perform a ritual harvesting of the mistletoe from the oak trees, clearing the path for the Oak King.

People would also bring evergreens inside, in much the same way we now set up Christmas trees—but in the case of Yule, the tree was never cut down. Instead, people brought in boughs of evergreen. The Yule log was a gigantic piece of wood that was either given as a gift by a friend or neighbor or harvested from the forest. It was traditionally ash, and it was often large enough to stick way out of the hearth, to be pushed in farther as it burned down. Once it was placed in the fire, the remaining portion was decorated with evergreens, holly, and ivy, doused with cider or ale, and finally dusted with flour, as representation of the work that had been done leading up to this night. The Yule fire itself was lit using a piece of the previous year's Yule log, saved just for this purpose.

WAYS TO CELEBRATE

- Decorate your home with mistletoe for peace and love and with holly and ivy to show your respect for the Holly King and the protection he offers.

- Make a Yule log, even if it's not large enough to stretch out into your living room. Toss some flour on it to represent what you've accomplished this winter, and be sure to save a piece for next year.

- Light a candle just as the sun goes down on this longest night, to keep the light with you through the dark.

Montol

THE WINTER SOLSTICE

Montol is quite a new festival, dating back to only 2007. On the other hand, you might argue that it has been around since the early 1800s, with a similar carnival atmosphere. And of course midwinter or solstice festivals in Europe hark back to much more ancient times than that. The creation of the Montol festival was part of a concerted effort in Cornwall to revive old traditions and practices, merging several customs together into this event.

Montol is distinct from Yule and celebrated very differently. Rather than focusing on the solstice because of its astronomical and harvest implications, December 21 was chosen because it is the traditional feast day of St. Thomas the Apostle, the so-called "Doubting Thomas" who needed to see and feel Jesus's wounds to believe in the resurrection.

The major feature of Montol is guise dancing, and everyone participates. There are several traditional directions you could go with your disguise, including:

◆ Mock formal, in which you wear your fanciest hand-me-downs as a way to mock the rich

◆ Rags and ribbons, which is sort of at the opposite end of the spectrum, but these rags tend to be quite fancy and elaborate

◆ Animals, including bulls, horses, and deer

◆ Dressing as a different gender

◆ Masks, but not character masks—so no Spidermen, but instead, a carnival masque or a lace veil

Whatever guise you choose, the idea is to go topsy-turvy with it. *Montol* translates from the Cornish to "balance," and so this festival is about flipping yourself over and trying on another identity for the night. The guise dance itself is informal and a bit chaotic, which is fitting. Early in the evening, a Lord of Misrule is chosen from among the revelers, and they lead the procession to the bonfire, where the dancing continues as the sun sets for the long night.

At around 10 p.m., someone from the crowd is chosen to "chalk the mock"—to draw a stick figure on a Yule log. The mock is then thrown on the bonfire to symbolize the death of the old year and the birth of the new.

WAYS TO CELEBRATE

◆ Add some chaos to your midwinter celebrations! Dressing up as something in opposition to your "usual" identity is a fun way to explore other ways of being.

◆ Designate a Lord of Misrule, and see what havoc you can wreak and what fun you can have.

◆ Chalk the mock! Draw a symbol on a log before tossing it into a bonfire. It doesn't have to be a stick figure—you can draw a representation of whatever you want to release with the death of the old year.

Kwanzaa

A SEVEN-DAY CELEBRATION BETWEEN DECEMBER 26 AND JANUARY 1

Kwanzaa is a more recent holiday than many others in this book, though it is rooted in harvest festival traditions in much of Africa. It was created by Maulana Karenga, an activist and black nationalist, in 1966. He wanted to "give blacks an alternative to the existing holiday of Christmas and . . .

an opportunity to celebrate themselves and their history, rather than simply imitate the practice of the dominant society."

Karenga established the Nguzo Saba, or the seven principles of Kwanzaa, and each day is dedicated to a specific principle.

DAY 1 ◆ UMOJA
(Unity) within the family, community, nation, and race

DAY 2 ◆ KUJICHAGULIA
(Self-Determination), so that Black people will
define and name themselves and speak with their own voice

DAY 3 ◆ UJIMA
(Collective Work and Responsibility), to work together
to solve community issues

DAY 4 ◆ UJAMAA
(Cooperative Economics), to build and support
Black businesses

DAY 5 ◆ NIA
(Purpose), so that all that we do is with the
purpose of restorative justice

DAY 6 ◆ KUUMBA
(Creativity) in all that we do to
support the community

DAY 7 ◆ IMANI
(Faith) in ourselves and each other

There are a variety of symbols associated with celebrations of Kwanzaa, which are placed on a mkeka, or mat, including a selection of crops like corn and a Kikombe cha Umoja, or unity cup, meant to be shared among family and friends, to give thanks. A Kinara holds seven candles, and one candle is lit for each night. Families will exchange gifts—often handmade—and will decorate with kente cloths. On the last evening, there is a feast.

WAYS TO CELEBRATE

◆ Even if we are not Black, we can all participate in supporting the Black community, particularly with regard to the tenets of Kwanzaa. On each day, consider how you can contribute.

◆ While Kwanzaa is celebrated after the majority of Western winter holidays, consider making your Christmas, Hanukkah, or other celebratory purchases with Ujamaa in mind, and support Black-owned businesses.

◆ Kwanzaa is a thoughtful holiday, meant to inspire participants to look forward to an improved future and to look backward at the support and struggles of ancestors. Again, this is something we can all do.

Hogmanay

JANUARY 1

If you've ever wondered why we sing Robert Burns's "Auld Lang Syne" at New Year's, the reason is Hogmanay. This New Year celebration in Scotland derives from Nordic and Celtic celebrations of the winter solstice, but unlike most ancient solstice celebrations, it has continued on without interruption into the modern day. This may perhaps be because in Scotland after the Protestant Reformation, Christmas was not celebrated as a holiday (too "papist"), and people needed to do *something* to break the monotony of winter. In anticipation of the new year, people would clean house, remove ashes from the fireplace, and clear all debts, both monetary and otherwise, as they prepared for a fresh start.

As with the Vietnamese spring festival Têt, the ritual of "first foot" is a big part of Hogmanay. It is an honor to be chosen to be the first guest to enter a household on Hogmanay, and a dark-haired man is the ideal choice. Whatever the reason for that, dark-haired men are in high demand on Hogmanay, and after midnight they go round to the houses of their friends and families, bringing salt, coal, shortbread, whiskey, and a kind of fruitcake called black bun—each of these gifts bestows luck on the household.

A slightly more alarming ritual is the swinging of fireballs on Hogmanay. The balls are up to two feet in diameter and formed of chicken wire, which is then filled with old newspapers, sticks, and other flammable materials. The balls are tired to a wire or chain about three feet long, and then set alight at midnight. The swingers parade through the streets of the town, tossing the burning balls about their heads.

Come New Year's morning, farmers would bless their livestock by sprinkling water collected from a "dead and living ford"—a river crossing that both the dead and the living use. They would sprinkle every member of the household, every bed, and every room, and then close the windows and light branches of juniper on fire, letting the smoke cleanse the space. Once the house is thoroughly smoky and unpleasant, they would fling open the doors and windows, inviting in the fresh air of the new year. Everyone shares a wee dram of whiskey, and then sits down to breakfast.

Given all this merrymaking, Scotland has declared January 2 a national holiday to give everyone a bit more time to recover.

WAYS TO CELEBRATE

◆ Choose a first foot for New Year's day, a special guest you feel a strong connection with—whatever their hair color might be.

◆ Collect water from a dead or living ford, and use it to bless your home and family.

◆ Learn the lyrics to "Auld Lang Syne" and celebrate its meaning—sharing joy and memory and a bit of whiskey with the people you love.

Lohri

JANUARY 13

Lohri is technically a winter solstice event, though it is not celebrated until the end of the solstice month, per the lunisolar Vikrami calendar.

It is also a harvest festival, as sugarcane and radish are gathered at this time of year. As a result, many sugarcane products are consumed, including jaggery (concentrated cane juice) and gachak (peanut brittle made with jaggery). Lohri marks the beginning of a new year for Punjabi farmers, and so they offer their thanks for the harvest and pray for a year of abundance by chanting "Aadar aye dilather aye," or "may honor come and poverty vanish."

Celebrations of Lohri are linked to Dulla Bhatti, a kind of Punjabi Robin Hood. He would steal from the rich and give to the poor, and he would rescue Hindu girls who had been kidnapped to be sold into slavery, and part of Lohri rituals involve children going door-to-door, singing a call-and-response song with the adults who answer. Afterward, the children are given sweets and treats, money, and logs for the Lohri bonfire. Sometimes, one of the children will be selected to be smeared with ash and tied with a rope around his waist. The idea is that if the adult does not offer enough, the rope will be loosened as a threat—and if the child escapes, they will run into the house to wreak destruction in revenge.

But the big event by far on Lohri is the bonfire. It is lit at sunset in the village square, and the children toss some—but probably not all—of their collected treats onto the fire, to represent the burning of the old year and the start of the next. It is believed that offering food to Lord Agni, the god of fire, will burn away negativity and create space for prosperity. People will also walk around the fire or dance around it, as they discard old ideas and thoughts that are no longer of use, and instead welcome in new ideas and good fortune.

WAYS TO CELEBRATE

◆ Make some gachak or other sugar-related food to celebrate the harvest.

◆ Invite family and friends to participate and seek offerings for the new year—if you have children in your life who can be a part of this, all the better!

◆ Light a bonfire, or even just a candle, and circle it, considering what thoughts or ideas you no longer wish to bring with you and what new thoughts and ideas you might want to invite in the new year.

Tu BiShvat

THE FIFTEENTH DAY OF THE HEBREW MONTH OF SHEVAT,
USUALLY IN JANUARY OR FEBRUARY

Tu BiShvat is both a Jewish holiday and an Israeli earth day—this "new year of the trees" is a way to celebrate life and the gifts the earth has to offer us. Back in the Middle Ages, Tu BiShvat was celebrated with a feast of fruits, and that seder is still sometimes performed today, mostly in Israel.

In the sixteenth century, Kabbalist Rabbi Yitzchak Luria established a Tu BiShvat seder, giving fruits and trees symbolic meaning related to the Tree of Life. In Jewish mysticism, it is believed that all physical forms carry a spark of the Divine, and the rituals of Tu BiShvat were intended to release these sparks, increasing God's presence on earth. The seder is performed as follows:

THE FIRST CUP ◆ This cup is to be filled with white wine or grape juice and symbolizes winter and the place from which God's energy infuses us with life.

THE FIRST FRUIT ◆ The first fruits to be consumed should have a hard shell on the outside, with a soft inside—like walnuts, coconuts, or almonds. The hard shell symbolizes the protection we receive from the earth.

THE SECOND CUP ◆ The second cup is filled with white wine, but with a drop or two of red to symbolize the changing of the seasons, and the ways in which creation is connected to water.

THE SECOND FRUIT ◆ The second fruit is a reverse of the first—in this case, there is a soft outside and a hard inside, as with olives, dates, peaches, and so forth. The pit symbolizes the life we receive from the earth and the strength we all carry within us.

THE THIRD CUP ◆ The third cup of wine is red, with a drop or two of white, furthering the change in the seasons and the progress of life.

THE THIRD FRUIT ◆ The third fruit is soft and entirely edible, including figs and grapes, and symbolizes the presence of God on earth.

THE FOURTH CUP ◆ The final cup of wine is entirely red, exploring the element of fire and celebrating the spark of God we all contain.

THE FOURTH FRUIT ◆ The final fruit is tough but not hard on the outside, and sweet within, like citrus, banana, avocado, and so forth. It symbolizes the mysteries of the Divine and the ways in which we are always seeking to uncover and learn.

Nowadays, Tu BiShvat is more often considered an environmentalist celebration, focusing on the reforesting of Israel, and a responsible ending to the earth.

WAYS TO CELEBRATE

◆ You can express your gratitude for the blessings of the earth by planting a tree, working in a community garden, or donating to environmental activist organizations.

◆ Whatever our religion, we can all feel a spark of *something*, whether it is God or the Divine or simply that bit of magic that makes us who we are. Take this day to experience that connection, that spark you carry.

◆ Use the Tu BiShvat seder as inspiration for a ritual of your own that symbolizes the changing of the seasons and the support and nourishment we receive from the earth.

Imbolc

FEBRUARY 1

Imbolc, also known as St. Brigid's Day, is a Celtic festival that dates back to ancient times. It is set at the midpoint between the winter solstice and the spring equinox and as such marks the beginning of the end of winter. Much like Groundhog Day in the United States, there is even a tradition of observing the behavior of wild animals—in this case, badgers and snakes—to see if they come out of their dens, foretelling an early spring.

People would also watch for the Cailleach, the hag queen of winter in the Celtic pantheon. If she has cast a bright and sunny day on Imbolc, then that means she is using this day to gather firewood, presaging a long winter. But if Imbolc is cold and stormy, then the Cailleach is asleep and winter will soon come to an end.

With the nearing of spring, farmers would begin to focus their attention on their livestock, working to ensure that the lambs were born so that the ewe's milk would come. This might seem trivial, but this kind of timing was the farmer's livelihood. As such, Imbolc was dedicated to the goddess Brigid, ruler of domesticated animals as well as wisdom, poetry, healing, protection, and blacksmithing—a goddess who, with the onset of Christianity, transformed into St. Brigid. Interestingly, one of the stories about St. Brigid is that she acted as a wet nurse for Christ as a baby.

On the eve of Imbolc, Brigid was welcomed into people's homes. They would leave bits of cloth outdoors for her to bless, imbuing them with protecting properties. They would prepare a special meal, serving colcannon, dumplings, and bannocks, making sure to set some aside for Brigid, and creating a bed for her out of hay or rushes. They would make a Brideogs, or a little doll made out of corn, and place it in the bed with a tiny birch wand. In some parts of Ireland, a family member would take on the role of Brigid and circle the home three times, carrying rushes, and then knock three times, asking to be let in. At the third knock, they would be welcomed inside and offered food, while the rushes would be made into a bed for the person playing Brigid. They would also make Brigid's crosses out of rushes tied or woven together and hang them over doors and windows to welcome Brigid and beseech her protection.

Today, Imbolc is celebrated by Wiccans, pagans, and Celtic peoples around the world, and by Christians as St. Brigid's Day. They make Brideogs and Brigid's crosses, dancing and singing, and setting their intentions for the coming spring.

WAYS TO CELEBRATE

◆ Venture out into nature to look for signs of the end of winter. If you don't particularly want to peer into a snake hole, look for bursting crocuses or the general movement of squirrels and chipmunks.

◆ Make Brideogs and bannocks, and build a bed for Brigid, so she will feel welcome.

◆ Craft a Brigid's cross and hang it over your windows for protection.

Mardi Gras

FORTY-SEVEN DAYS BEFORE EASTER SUNDAY,
USUALLY FEBRUARY OR MARCH

Mardi Gras is a carnival celebrating the beginning of Lent, a period of fasting and abstention observed in various Christian denominations. It occurs on Shrove Tuesday, also known as Fat Tuesday, and is essentially a time for people to go hog wild before plunging into the austerities of Lent. While most places in the world observe Mardi Gras for only a few days, in New Orleans it lasts for weeks, stretching from Twelfth Night (the Twelfth Day of Christmas) to Ash Wednesday (the day after Shrove Tuesday).

It's possible that this festival was once linked with Saturnalia, an ancient Roman pagan rite, which, like so many others, was folded into Christianity. Saturnalia was held around the winter solstice and was pretty much ritual mayhem. In addition, enslavers would wait upon enslaved peoples, and one of the enslaved would be elected the King of Saturnalia, presiding over the revels.

The largest Mardi Gras celebration in the United States is in New Orleans, but it didn't start there. Mardi Gras made its way to North America from France, with the first American celebration occurring in 1703. By the late 1800s it became the masked bacchanal it is today, with parades of secretive clubs called krewes with their elaborate floats and masks, off of which "throws" were offered to the watching crowds. These were usually beads, but can include cups, stuffed animals, and even shoes. In 1872, a group of businessmen came up with the idea of resurrecting the king—in this case the king of Carnival, or Rex. The first Rex was visiting Russian Grand Duke Alexis Romanoff—which is why the Romanoff family colors of purple, green, and gold are now the official colors of Mardi Gras. In 1892, another Rex gave the colors meanings: purple is for justice, green is for faith, and gold is for power.

New Orleans is known for its food and music, and Mardi Gras is no exception to that. Jazz and zydeco, rhythm and blues, and second line music echo throughout the city. Red beans and rice, jambalaya, po'boys, and hurricanes will keep everyone's energy up, but the most famous food served during Mardi Gras is the king cake. These treats are traditionally Bundt cakes baked with a tiny baby inside—and whoever gets the slice with the baby is responsible for purchasing the next king cake, week after week throughout Mardi Gras season.

New Orleans Mardi Gras has so many krewes and parades that, during Mardi Gras season, it can be hard to drive down a street without running into a parade. But one of the most complex and intriguing subcultures of Mardi Gras is the tradition of Mardi Gras Indians. These tribes are influenced by the history of both enslaved Africans and the friendship they forged with Native Americans. At certain points in Mardi Gras history, Black people were not allowed to participate in the celebrations—so they held a separate Carnival in their own, segregated neighborhoods. There are over forty Mardi Gras Indians tribes, including the Young Maasai Hunters, the Wild Tchoupitoulas, and the Bayou Renegades. Each tribe is hierarchical, with positions including Big Chief, Big Queen, Spy Boy, and Flag Boy, with their own responsibilities. Each tribe will create incredibly elaborate and intricate suits that take the entire year to put together, cost thousands of dollars, and weigh up to 150 pounds. Mardi Gras Indian parades are never announced in advance, and so you have to be paying attention and exploring the city to catch them.

WAYS TO CELEBRATE

◆ Throw a bacchanal of your own! Bake a king cake, play some amazing music, wear masks, and go wild and free.

◆ Get crafty! A big part of Mardi Gras culture involves creating an elaborate work of art. You could decorate masks, make costumes, and definitely work in some purple, green, and gold.

◆ Designate a Rex for the day, someone who perhaps doesn't normally speak up or make a lot of decisions. Give them permission to lean into that authority.

Conclusion

THERE IS A DEEP SENSE OF HISTORY IN THESE RITUALS, in the knowledge that some of them have been practiced for hundreds and thousands of years. And yet we are still creating new ones, finding new reasons to celebrate the earth and its changing seasons. While we have moved out of agrarian societies and are no longer so dependent on the seasons for harvest, we are energetically moved and changed by the shifting and twirling of the earth.

We can learn from each other, find inspiration and affinity with the rituals performed by people we have never met and the magics that can expand our awareness and understanding of ourselves and our place in the cycles of nature.

However you choose to engage with the seasons and the rituals that have been developed to celebrate them over the course of human history, there is comfort and inspiration to be found in the knowledge that we are all so deeply connected. We may speak different languages and follow different traditions, but we value the same things—connection with the earth, with our ancestors, and with each other.

Acknowledgments

First and foremost, I have to thank my dad for coming up with the idea for this book. Who knew that being lazy and pouring red wine into a glass of white wine would spark such a project? I loved learning so much while writing this book, particularly during a time when we've all been feeling so isolated. It's comforting to know how much we all have in common, wherever we are.

Dave, Maile, Annie, Mom, Dad, and Hannah—you are all the best. Let's go experience some rituals someday.

Shannon Fabricant, thank you for always being there, for your flexibility and your dedication. Big love.

To Shannon Kelly, thank you so much for stepping in whenever you are needed. Thank you always and forever to Susan Van Horn, genius designer and all-around good human. Thank you to Bárbara Tamilin—yay! I'm so excited to get to work with you and your vibrant, stunning art. Thank you to Amber Morris for always keeping the ship running smoothly, and to Ashley Benning—I feel like I know you, and I trust you implicitly. Thank you to Kristin Kiser, Francesca Begos and the foreign rights team, and to Amy Cianfrone, Valerie Howlett, Isabella Nugent, and Kara Thornton and everyone in the publicity and marketing teams—you are all incredible, and I owe you everything.

Index

A

Ama Nowruz, 24
Ancestral altar, 64–65
Armenia, 54–55

B

Baba Marta Day, 16–17
Bathukamma, 78–79
Beltane, 37–39
Bon (Obon), 57–58
Brazil, 50
Brideogs, 127
Bulgaria, 16, 52

C

Cambodian Water Festival, 90–91
Candle spell, 96–97
Chaharshanbe Suri, 23–24
Chang'e, 71–73
Chaos magic, 98–99
Chichen Itza, 26
China
    Chinese New Year, 10–12
    Dongzhi, 104–5
    Moon Festival, 71–72
    Qingming Festival, 34–36
Christmas rituals, 109–11
Cow Festival, 69–70

D

Día de Muertos, 86–88
Diwali, 80–83
Dongzhi, 104–5
Duke Wen, 35

E

Eggs
    balancing, 12
    magic spell, 8–9
    symbolism, 27–28, 33
Egypt, 32
Enyovden, 52
Eostre/Easter, 27–28
Estonia, 52

F

Fall equinox, 74–75
Fall rituals
    about, 63
    ancestral altar, 64–65
    Bathukamma, 78–79
    Día de Muertos, 86–88
    Diwali, 80–83
    fall equinox, 74–75
    Gai Jatra, 69–70
    Homowo, 67–68
    Loi Krathong, 89–91
    Mabon, 74–75
    Makahiki, 92–93
    Moon Festival, 71–73
    moon meditation, 66
    Samhain, 84–85
    Sukkot, 76–77
Festival of Lights, 80–83
Finland, 52
Floralia, 37–39
Flower dyeing spell, 44–45
"Four Kinds," 77

G

Gai Jatra, 69–70
Gauri, 78–79
Ghana, 67
Ghost Festival, 56–58
Great Dragon Parade, 40–41

H

Halloween, 85
Hawaii, 92–93
Hindu Festival of Colors, 18–21
Hiranyakashipu, 19
Hogmanay, 118–20
Holi, 18–21
Holly King, 110
Homowo, 67–68

I

Iceland, 110
Imbolc, 126–28
India, 18
Inti Raymi, 106–8
Ireland, 59–60, 110
Ivan Kupala, 52–53

J

Jaanipäev, 52
Japan, 57–58

K

Kachinas, 100–101
Kapila Brahma, 29–30
Karnak Temple, 48
Krakus, 40
Krathong, 89–90
Krishna, 18–19
Kwanzaa, 115–17

L

Lammas (Loaf-Mass), 60
Lent, 129
Lichun, 10–12
Litha, 47–49
Lohri, 121–22
Loi Krathong, 89–91
Love spell, 46
Lughnasadh, 59–60

M

Mabon, 74–75
Maias, 38

Makahiki, 92–93
Mardi Gras, 129–31
Martenitsi, 16–17
Mary's Day, 39
Maudgalyayana, 56–57
Maulana Karenga, 115–16
May Day, 37–39
Mesoamerican spring
    equinox, 25–26
Mexico, 25–26, 86–87
Midsummer, 50–53
Mistletoe, 110–11
Montol, 112–14
Moon Festival, 71–73
Moon meditation, 66

N

Nane Sarma, 24
Nepal, 18, 69
New year rituals
    Chinese, 10–12
    Hogmanay, 118–20
    Vietnamese, 13–15
Nowruz, 22–24

O

Oak King, 47–49
Ostara, 27–28

P

Palace of Quetzalcoatl,
    25–26
Poland, 40–41
Portugal, 38, 50

Prince Chong'er, 34–35
Pyramid of the Sun,
    25–26

Q

Qingming Festival,
    34–36
Quetzalcoatl, 25–26

R

Radha, 18–19
Rituals. *See also specific
    seasons*
    inspiration from, 133
    overview, 1–2

S

Samhain, 84–85
Santos Populares, 50
Scotland, 118–20
Seder, Tu BiShvat, 123–25
Serbia, 16
Sham el-Nessim, 32–33
Slavic countries, 52
Songkran, 29–31
South Korea, 105
Soyal, 100–101
Spells
    candle, 96–97
    egg, 8–9
    flower dyeing, 44–45
    love, 46
Spring rituals
    about, 5

Baba Marta Day, 16–17
Beltane, 37–39
Chinese New Year,
   10–12
egg spell, 8–9
Great Dragon Parade,
   40–41
Holi, 18–21
Mesoamerican spring
   equinox, 25–26
Nowruz, 22–24
Ostara, 27–28
Qingming Festival,
   34–36
Sham el-Nessim,
   32–33
Songkran, 30
spring cleaning ritual,
   6–7
spring equinox, 22–28
Têt, 13–15
St. Brigid's Day, 126–28
St. John's Day, 50–51
Stonehenge, 48
Sukkot, 76–77

Summer rituals
   about, 43
   flower dyeing spell,
      44–45
   Ghost Festival, 56–58
   Litha, 47–49
   love spell, 46
   Lughnasadh, 59–60
   Midsummer, 50–53
   summer solstice, 47–49
   Vardavar, 54–55

T
Taiwan, 105
Temple of Kukulcán, 25
Temple of the Sun, 48
Têt, 13–15
Thailand, 89
Thammabal, 29–30
Tu BiShvat, 123–25

V
Vardavar, 54–55
Vietnam, 13–15
Vishnu, 19

W
Walpurgis, 38
Wawel Dragon, 40–41
Winter rituals
   about, 95
   candle spell, 96–97
   chaos magic, 98–99
   Dongzhi, 104–5
   Hogmanay, 118–20
   Imbolc, 126–28
   Inti Raymi, 106–8
   Kwanzaa, 115–17
   Lohri, 121–22
   Mardi Gras, 129–31
   Montol, 112–14
   Soyal, 100–101
   Tu BiShvat, 123–25
   winter solstice, 100–114
   Yaldā, 102–3
   Yule, 109–11

Y
Yaldā, 102–3
Yi Peng, 90
Yule, 109–11